A
LARGE DESCRIPTION
OF GALLOWAY,

BY ANDREW SYMSON,

MINISTER OF KIRKINNER,

M.DC.LXXX.IV.

WITH AN APPENDIX,

CONTAINING ORIGINAL PAPERS,

FROM THE

SIBBALD AND MACFARLANE

MSS.

EDINBURGH:
PRINTED FOR W. AND C. TAIT.
M.DCCC.XXIII.

A Large Description Of Galloway,

Andrew Symson

A

LARGE DESCRIPTION

OF GALLOWAY.

TABLE OF CONTENTS.

PAGE.

NOTICE . . . . , . . . V

DESCRIPTION OF GALLOWAY.

Advertisement by the Author 3
Introduction 5
Stewartry of Kirkcudburgh 7
Shire of Wigton 33
Answers to Queries concerning Galloway . . 70

APPENDIX.

I. Galloway typographised by Mr Timothy Pont . 111
II. Description of the Stewartrie of Kirkcudbright 118
III. Description of the Parish of Kirkpatrick Durham, 125
IV. Description of the Parish of Minigaff . 132
V. Description of the Sheriffdom of Wigton . 144
VI. Farther Account of Galloway, by Dr Archbald 149
VII. Description of the Bounds of the Presbytery of
Penpont 151
VIII. Dedication of Symson's *Tripatriarchichon* . 170
IX. Preface to Symson's *Tripatriarchichon* . 177
X. *Funeral Elegies*, by Symson . . . 189

NOTICE.

ANDREW SYMSON, the author of the following *Description of Galloway*, was a Curate of the Scottish Episcopal Church. He was Minister of the Parish of Kirkinner, in Wigtonshire, for upwards of twenty years prior to the Revolution. Little is known of his personal history, previous to the commencement of his ministry. We have his own authority for stating, that he received a university education, and was the *condisciple* of Alexander Earl of Galloway, who succeeded to his title and estates in 1671.[1] It is probable that Symson formed an early intimacy with this nobleman, under the pa-

[1] Dedication to *Tripatriarchichon*. Appendix, No. VIII.

tronage of whose father, Earl James, it may
be presumed, he was introduced into the parish of Kirkinner about 1663. Long after
losing his incumbency,[1] he speaks of his lot
there as having been " cast in a very pleasant
place."[2] Not that he was exempted from the
persecutions of the dark time during which
his ministry lasted. In 1679, when the public acknowledgment of an Episcopal clergy-
man in Scotland was looked upon as a crime,
Symson informs us, that he was " necessitate
to retire to a quiet lurking place."[3] The
family of Galloway did not desert him in this
the day of his distress. Earl Alexander received him into his house, where he was pro-
tected and treated with the greatest kindness.

His congregation, however, gradually deserted him, and his *hearers* were at length

---

[1] 1705.
[2] Preface to *Tripatriarchichon*. Appendix, No. IX.
[3] Appendix, No. VIII.

reduced to two or three. Among these, he speaks with much affection of David Dunbar, younger of Baldone, only son of Sir David Dunbar of Baldone, Baronet. This gentleman lost his life by a fall from his horse on the 20th of March, 1682, in riding between Leith and Holyrood-House. He was commemorated in a *Funeral Elegie* by Symson, which contains the following lines :—

" In th' late Rebellion, that unhappy time
When loyalty was look'd on as a crime,
And Royalists were hooted at like owles,
Esteem'd deserving nought but scoffs and scowles,
Frowns, mocks, and taunts, of which HE had his share ;
(And 'twas my daily bread, and constant fare ;)
In that unhappy time, I say, when I
Was almost drown'd in deep perplexity,
When many persons would no longer stay,
And all my summer birds fled quite away ;
Yet he (brave soul) did always constant prove ;
My change of fortune never changed his love ;
For change who lik'd, he ever was the same ;
In nothing chang'd, save that he chang'd his name.
His name was only chang'd, but not the man ;
I was the *David*, he the *Jonathan*.
   He was no schismatick, he ne'er withdrew
Himself from th' House of God ; he with a few

(Some two or three) came constantly to pray
For such as had withdrawn themselves away.
Nor did he come by fits ; foul day or fair,
I, being i'th' church, was sure to see him there.
Had he withdrawn, 'tis like these two or three,
Being thus discourag'd, had deserted me.
So that my muse 'gainst *Priscian* avers
He, HE alone, WERE my parishioners,
Yea, and my constant hearers ! Oh ! that I
Had pow'r to eternize his memory,
Then (though my joy, my glory, and my crown,
By this unhappy fall be thus fall'n down,)
I'd rear an everlasting monument,
A curious structure of a large extent,
A brave and stately pile, that should out-bid
Egyptian Cheops's costly Pyramid ;
A monument that should outlive the blast
Of time and malice too ; a pile should last
Longer than hardest marble, and surpass
The bright and durable Corinthian brass."

In the remainder of this Elegy, David
Dunbar is described as an active country gentleman, and a well-educated, intelligent scholar,—possessing an amiable and affectionate disposition, and on many trying occasions acting as the *bosom friend* of his persecuted minister.

About the period of the Revolution, Sym-

son retired to Edinburgh, where he became
an author and a printer. His most elaborate
work is a poem, which he printed and published at Edinburgh in 1705, under the following title :—TRIPATRIARCHICON; *or, the*
Lives of the three Patriarchs, Abraham,
Isaac, and Jacob, extracted forth of the
Sacred Story, and digested into English
verse by ANDREW SYMSON, M.A., *and then*
Minister of Kirkinner. Little can be said in
commendation of the poetry of this volume.
Indeed, in a *Funeral Elegie* upon the death of
Sir Alexander M'Culloch of Myrtoun, Baronet, *qui vi et injuria aquarum periit, Junii*
3, 1675, Symson thus apologises for the de-
fects of his *rustick muse* :—

   " I never was in Greece ; never did behold
   The Muses comely walk, describ'd of old
   By such as knew it well ; I never saw
   The famous Hippocrene, digg'd by the claw
   Or hoof of winged Pegasus ; not I.
   Alas ! I never was admitted to come nigh
   The same by many stages, or tread on
   The pleasant way that leads to Helicon.

I never drank of the pure crystall fountain,
Nor ever slept on the renown'd mountain
Of fork't Parnassus : No, my Muse was bred
In a cold climate, and I rest my head
Beneath Arcturus and his sons"——

The *Dedication* and *Preface*[1] to the *Tripatriarchicon* are curious, and disclose a variety of particulars regarding the Author. The former is addressed to James, Earl of Galloway, the son of Symson's patron, Earl Alexander——the latter to the reader. The *Dedication* contains a short genealogical account of the family of Galloway, and in addition to the particulars already mentioned respecting the patronage and protection of Symson by Earl Alexander, he informs us in this piece, that, after he left Kirkinner, two of Earl James's younger brothers were entrusted to the care of his son as a tutor. In the *Preface* to his poem, Symson gives a sketch of the ecclesiastical state of Galloway

[1] Appendix, No. VIII. IX.

during the period of his incumbency, which
will be found far from uninteresting. It is
written in a very pleasing and amiable tone,
and conveys a most favourable impression of
the character and intelligence of the author—
breathing, in all its allusions to the distracted
state of the country, much of that resigned
spirit, in which he remarks, towards the commencement of his *Description of Galloway*,
that he was a residenter in the parish of
Kirkinner, " by the providence of God, and
the protection of his Sacred Majestie's laws,
for more than twentie years, *per varios casus, et per discrimina rerum.*"[1]

Symson was also the author of several
Elegies. The Editor is not aware of the
precise period at which they were printed.

[1] In 1707, Symson printed a small volume, entitled
" ΔΕΥΤΕΡΟΣΚΟΠΙΑ ; *or a brief Discourse concerning
the Second Sight, commonly so called ; by John Fraser,
Minister of Teree and Coll, and Dean of the Isles:
Published by Mr Andrew Symson, with a short Account
of the Author.*"

They are of considerable rarity, and he has only seen one copy, which was most politely communicated to him by Sir Walter Scott. It is bound up with the *Tripatriarchichon* ; but has no title-page, and bears no date. The two first Elegies are upon Archbishop Sharpe and Sir George M'Kenzie of Rosehaugh, King's Advocate during the reigns of Charles the Second and James the Second. The remaining Elegies, eleven in number, are intended to commemorate different persons connected with the Shire of Wigton. Of these, in addition to the lines already quoted from the Elegies upon David Dunbar of Baldone, and Sir Alexander M'Culloch of Myrtoun, a specimen will be found in the Appendix.[1]

During Symson's residence at Kirkinner, a series of queries was extensively circulated in Scotland by Sir Robert Sibbald, for the purpose of procuring information with a view

[1] No. X.

to the publication of a Scottish Atlas. This eminent person had previously obtained a patent from Charles the Second, to be his Majesty's Geographer for the kingdom of Scotland; and in a manuscript account of his life, preserved in the Library of the Faculty of Advocates,[1] he informs us, that, " in order to the accomplishment of the description of the kingdome, I did, in the year 1682, publish in our language ane advertisement, and some generall queries, copies whereof were sent over all the kingdome."[2] These inquiries attracted the attention of Symson, who undertook the task of drawing up a general *Description of Galloway*. This he performed in 1684, and afterwards in 1692, when residing at Dalclathick, in Glenartney, carefully revised and enlarged his work. It is probable, that, soon after this period, the

[1] Jac. V. 6. 26.
[2] P. 38.

original manuscript was transmitted to Sir Robert Sibbald, who, in the account of his life already referred to, acknowledges to have received it.[1] Along with the other papers of that celebrated geographer, it was ultimately deposited in the Library of the Faculty of Advocates.

Although Symson's work has been often quoted and referred to, and although its *modest merits* have been generally acknowledged, it has hitherto been preserved in manuscript. An Edition of the *Description of Galloway* is now, for the first time, offered to the attention of the public. The interest of the work is no doubt in some degree *local*; but it will be found to contain much valuable information respecting the Geography, Natural History, Agriculture, and Statistics of Galloway, accompanied by an Account of the Manners and Customs of the Inhabitants, towards the

[1] P. 38.

close of the seventeenth century. Of these no authentic memorials are to be found elsewhere ; and it becomes therefore desirable to give to Symson's authentic record of them, a more accessible and imperishable form than it has hitherto possessed. The minute geographical details in the *Description of Galloway* are frequently inaccurate. Nor is this remarkable ; as it is more than probable, that Symson described the boundaries of the different parishes, rather from the reports of others, than from his own observation. This remark, however, does not apply to the other parts of his work, which are in all respects original and authentic.

An Appendix has been subjoined to the *Description of Galloway*, containing several unpublished papers connected with that district, which have been extracted from manuscripts preserved in the Library of the Faculty of Advocates, and which, it is thought, will add in some degree to the value of the present volume. The orthography of the manuscripts, however unsystematic and irregular, has been adhered to.

EDINBURGH,
M.DCCC.XXIII.

A
LARGE DESCRIPTION
OF GALLOWAY,

BY

MR. ANDREW SYMSON.

ADVERTISEMENT

BY

THE AUTHOR.

Such passages as relate to time or persons
are to be understood with respect to the year
1684, in which year these Papers were at first
form'd ; severall of them being only writen
in short notes, which were to have been afterwards extended ; but the troubles, which very
shortly thereafter did ensue, occasion'd these
Papers to be cast by, yea, and almost wholy
forgotten, for some yeares. Being at length
desired to extend and transcribe the same, I
severall times set about it, but was diverted ;
however, having here time and leasure enough,
I have transcribed them : wherein are insert-

ed, here and there, severall particulars, which were either wholy omitted at first, or of which I had not then so full information as I have since procur'd from many persons, on severall occasions.

DALCLATHICK, IN GLENARTNAE, June 28, 1692.

A LARGE DESCRIPTION

OF

GALLOWAY.

ADDRESSED TO SIR ROBERT SIBBALD.

INTRODUCTION.

Whereas there came lately to my hands some printed sheets, bearing title, *Nuncius Scoto-Britannus, sive Admonitio de Atlante Scotico, &c.* together with *An Account of the Scotish Atlas*, &c. subjoyn'd thereto, wherein it is desired that you may receave answers to severall queries emitted by you, or what other information can be had for the embellishment of that work, which you are to publish, in obedience to his Sacred Majestie's commands. I have judged it not altogether excentrical to my profession to comply something with my genius ; and therefore have drawn up this following information, which, although in generall it may serve for the whole tract of Galloway, and more particularly for the Shire of Wigton, yet it is chiefly calculated for the meridian of the presbytry of Wigton, in one of the parishes whereof I have, (by the providence of God, and the protection of his Sacred Majestie's laws,) for more than twentie yeares, been a residenter, *per varios casus, et per discrimina rerum.*

When I mention the distance of places, I would not be understood as speaking exactly, geometricaly, or in *rectâ lineâ*, but only according to the vulgar account, and as the countrey people do commonly estimate the same ; and so also, mentioning East, West, North, South, &c. I do not always mean, exactly according to that very point of the compas, but only that the place spoken of lyes towards that part, although it may be three or four points distant from the exact cardinal point made mention of.

The tract of ground call'd commonly by the name of Galloway, reacheth from the port, which is upon the bridge of Dumfriese, (under which the river of Nith runneth,) unto the Mule of Galloway, and extendeth, according to the vulgare estimation, to about threescore and four miles in length.

This tract of ground hath on the east Nithisdale ; on the south and west, it is environed with the sea ; on the north, it is bounded with the shire of Air, viz. Kyle and Carrick.

Although this whole tract hath the name of Galloway, yet it is not subject to one and the same jurisdiction, neither civil, nor ecclesiastical, nor consistorial.

We shall divide it with respect to its civil jurisdiction ; and as we speake particularly thereof, we shall also take notice of the other jurisdictions contained therein.

With reference to its civil jurisdiction, it is divided into the Stewartry of Kirkcudburgh, and the Shire of Wigton ; whereof the Stewartry exceeds the Shire both in bounds and valuation, being valued at $5 \div 8$ parts ; whereas the Shire is only valued at $3 \div 8$ parts.[1]

---

[1] Appendix, No. I.

PART FIRST.

STEWARTRY OF KIRKCUDBURGH.

THE Stewartry of Kirkcudburgh is bounded on the east with Nithisdale; on the south, with the sea; on the west, with the Shire of Wigton, and parted therefrom by the river of Cree; on the north, it is bounded partly with Kyle, partly with Carrick.[1]

The Stewartry of Kirkcudburgh contains twenty-eight principal parishes, viz.

1. TRAQUEER. The Bishop of Galloway is patron hereof; it being a pendicle of the Abbacy of Tougueland, of which more hereafter, when we shall have occasion to answer the querie concerning the revenues of the Bishoprick of Galloway. The parish-kirk is twenty-four miles distant from the town of Kirkcudburgh, and about a quarter of a mile distant from the town of Dumfreise. The parish of Traqueer is bounded on the east with the town, and parish of Dumfreise, from which it is separated by the river of Nith; on the south, it is bounded with the parish of New Abbey; on the west, with the

[1] Appendix, No. II.

parish of Lochruiton; and on the north-west, with the parish of Terregles.

2. NEW ABBEY. The Bishop of Edinburgh is patron hereof; which, with six other kirks depending thereon, viz. Kirkcudburgh, Bootle, Kelton, Corsemichael, Kirkpatrick, and Orr, (of all which more hereafter,) were formerly appointed for the maintaining of the Castle of Edinburgh; but when King Charles the Martyr thought fit to erect the Bishoprick of Edinburgh, his Majesty disjoyn'd the said kirk of New Abbey, with the other six kirks depending thereon, from the Castle of Edinburgh, and gave them to the Bishoprick of Edinburgh, towards the maintenance of the Bishop of that sea. The Kirk of New Abbey is twentie-four miles distant from the town of Kirkcudburgh, and five miles distant from the town of Dumfriese. The parish of New Abbey is bounded on the east with the parish of Karlaverock, (in the shire of Nithisdale,) from which it is separated by the river of Nith; on the south, it is bounded with the parish of Kirkbeen; on the west, with the parish of Kirkgunnion; on the north-west, with the parish of Lochruiton; and on the north, with the parish of Traqueir.

3. KIRKBEEN. Maxwell of Kirkhouse is patron hereof. The parish-kirk is twentie-four miles distant from the town of Kirkcudburgh, and nine miles distant from the town of Dumfreise. This kirk (with some others, of which more hereafter in the description of the parish of Terregles,) depended of old upon the Provestry of Lincluden. The parish of Kirkbeen is bounded on the east, partly with the parish of Karlaverock, (from which it is separated by the river of Nith,) and partly with the sea; on the south, it is bounded with the sea; on the southwest, with the parish of Suddick, (of which in the description of the parish of Cowend;) on the west, with the

parish of Kirkgunnion ; and on the north, with the parish of New Abbey.

4. COWEND. The Marquess of Queensberry is patron of this parish of Cowend, (which also of old depended on the Provestry of Lincluden, of which hereafter in the description of the parish of Terregles.) But there is another parish annext thereto, called Southwick, (pronounced Siddick or Suddick,) whereof the Bishop of Dumblain is patron. It belonging, as I suppose, to the Abbacy of Dundranan, (of which hereafter,) to which Abbacy the Bishop of Dumblain hath right, as Dean of his Majestie's chapel-royal. 'Tis said, that this Suddick is directly south from John-a-Groatis' house in Cathness. The parish-kirk of Cowend is thirteen miles distant from the town of Kirkcudburgh, and fourteen miles distant from the town of Dumfreise. The parish of Cowend, with the annext parish of Suddick, is bounded on the east with the parish of Kirkbeen ; on the south, with the sea ; on the west, partly with the parish of Orr, and partly with the parish of Bootle, (from which it is separated by the river of Orr,) and partly with the parish of Dundranan, (from which it is separated by ane arme of the sea ;) on the north, it is bounded with the parish of Kirkgunnion.

5. ORR. The Bishop of Edinburgh is patron hereof, as depending on New Abbey. The kirk of Orr is twelve miles distant from the town of Kirkcudburgh, and twelve miles distant from the town of Dumfreise. The parish of Orr is bounded eastwardly with the parish of Kirkgunnion ; on the south-east, with the parish of Cowend ; on the south-south-west, with the parishes of Bootle and Corsemichael, from both which parishes it is separated by the river of Orr ; on the north-west, it is bounded with the parish of Kirkpatrick Durham ; on the north,

with the parish of Irongray ; and on the north-east, it is bounded with the parish of Lochruiton.

6. KIRKPATRICK. This parish, to distinguish it from other Kirkpatricks, is called also Kirkpatrick Durham. The lands in this parish, belonging to M'Naight of Kilquonadie, pertained of old to the name of Durham. The Bishop of Edinburgh, as having a right to New Abbey, is patron of this parish. This kirk of Kirkpatrick Durham is thirteen miles distant from the town of Kirkcudburgh, and eleven miles distant from the town of Dumfreise. The parish of Kirkpatrick Durham is bounded, on the east, with Kirkpatrick Iron Gray ; on the south-east, with the parish of Orr ; on the south, it is bounded with the parish of Corsemichael, from which it is divided by the river of Orr ; on the south-west and westwardly, it is divided from the parish of Partan by the river of Orr ; on the north-west and westwardly, it is bounded with the parish of Balmaclellan, from which it is separated by the said river of Orr ; on the north, it is bounded, partly with the parish of Glencairn, within the shire of Nithisdale, and presbytry of Pinpont, and partly with the parish of Dunscore, within the shire of Nithisdale, and presbytry of Dumfreise.[1]

7. IRON GREY ; Called also Kirkpatrick Iron Grey. M'Brair of Newark is patron hereof. The parish-kirk of Iron Grey is twentie-three miles distant from the town of Kirkcudburgh, and three miles distant from the town of Dumfreise. This parish of Iron Grey is bounded, on the east, with the parish of Terregles ; on the south-east, with the parish of Lochruiton ; on the south, with the parish of Orr ; on the south-south-west, with the parish of Kirkpatrick Durham ; on the west and northwardly,

---

[1] Appendix, No. III.

with the parish of Dunscore; on the north-east and northwardly, with the parish of Holywood, in the shire of Nithisdale, and presbytry of Dumfreise, from which parish of Holywood to the north-east, this parish of Iron Grey is divided by the water of Cluden.

8. TERREGLES. Concerning the Latine name of it, one man told me it was *Terra Regalis;* another said it was *Tertia Ecclesia;* a third said it was *Terra Ecclesia;* so that it should be spell'd perhaps Tereglise. And as there is some debate concerning its name, so there is about its patronage; the Earl of Nithisdale, and the Marquess of Queensberry, each of them pretending thereto. Which of them hath the best right, I shall not take upon me to determine. However, the intrant, for his better securitie, doth commonly procure a presentation from each of them; but then again, the Archbishop of Glasgow comes in for his share, and pretends that *jus patronatus* belongs to him; and thereupon grants a presentation himselfe, and gives collation only thereupon. The parish-kirk is distant from the town of Kirkcudburgh twentie-three miles, and a large mile distant from the town of Dumfreise. It is but a small parish. It is bounded, on the east, with the parish of Dumfreise, and separated from it by the river of Nith; on the south-east, it is bounded with the parish of Traqueer; on the south and south-west, with the parish of Lochruiton; on the west, with the parish of Iron Gray; on the north, with the parish of Holywood, from which it is divided by the water of Cluden, which emptieth itselfe in the river of Nith. Neer to this water of Cluden, is a place called the Colledge or Provestry of Lincluden,[1] on which

---

[1] " LINCLUDAN, in the shire of Dumfries, was founded in the reign of King Malcolm IV. by Uthred, father to Rolland Lord of Galloway. *Alienore Priouresse de Lencluden del Conte de Dum-*

this parish of Terregles, together with the parishes of Kirkbeen, Cowend, and Lochruiton, together also with the parish of Karlaverock, in the shire of Nithisdale, did of old depend.

9. LOCHRUITON. The Marquess of Queensberry is patron hereof. It did of old depend upon the provestry of Lincluden, as hath been said in the description of the parish of Terregles. The parish-kirk is twenty miles distant from the town of Kirkcudburgh, and four miles distant from the town of Dumfreise. The parish of Lochruiton is bounded, on the east, with the parish of Traqueer; on the south-east, with the parish of New Abbey; on the south, with the parish of Kirkgunnion; on the south-west and westwardly, with the parish of Orr; on the north, with the parish of Iron Gray; on the north and north-east, with the parish of Terregles.

10. KIRKGUNNION; (Or Kirkgúnguent, as I am informed, *ab extrema unctione*, it being a pendicle of the Abbey of Holme, in Cumberland.) The Earl of Nithisdale is patron hereof. This parish-kirk is sixteen miles distant from the town of Kircudburgh, and eight miles distant from the town of Dumfreise. This parish is bounded, on the east, with the parish of New Abbey; on the south, with the two annext parishes of Suddick

fries, is mentioned by Prynne, *ad annum* 1296. This Priory was afterwards changed by Archibald the Grim, Earl of Douglas, and Lord of Galloway, into a College or Provostry, because of the lewd and scandalous lives of the Nuns."—SPOTISWOOD'S *Religious Houses*, Chap. XVIII. § 2. No. 5.

" LINCLUDEN, in Galloway, situate upon the Water of Cluden, where it falls into the river Nith, some few miles above Dumfries, was formerly a cloister of Black Nuns, as is above related. But it was afterwards changed into a Provostry by Archibald the Grim, Earl of Douglas, in the reign of King Robert III. *Magister Alexander de Carnys, Præpositus de Lincludan*, is designed by Archibald Lord Galloway, *Cancellarius Noster*, in a charter dated the 12th February, 1413."—*Ibid.* Chap. XIX. § 20.

and Cowend; on the south-west and westwardly, with the parish of Orr; and on the north, with the parish of Lochruiton.

As to the ecclesiastical jurisdiction of these ten parishes, (being commonly called the ten kirks beneath Orr,) they ly within the diocese of Glasgow, and are subjected to the care of the Archbishop thereof, and under him are a part of the presbytry of Dumfreis, and belong thereunto. These parishes also (excepting Kirkgunnion) belong to the jurisdiction of the Commissary of Dumfreise, who also hath his dependance upon the Archbishop of Glasgow. But as for Kirkgunnion, it is a distinct Commissariot within itselfe, where the Earl of Nithisdale is heritable Commissary; but from whom the said Earl derives his authority, I know not. The reason why it is a distinct Commissariot within itselfe, and independent upon any bishop of Scotland, seems to be this: Because, as said is, it being a pendicle of the Abbey of Holm, in Cumberland; and no Scottish bishop hath any right to the said Abbey, and consequently hath no right to the Commissariot in Kirkgunnion, which is, as hath been said, a pendicle thereof.

11. KIRKCUDBURGH. So called from the kirk dedicated to St Cudbert. It hath two other kirks annext thereto, viz. Galtway, (pronounced Gaata,) where Lidderdail of Isle hath his interest; and Dunrod, appertaining to Sir David Dunbar of Baldone. Kirkcudburgh is the head burgh of the Stewartry, being about twenty-four miles from Dumfreis westward, and about sixteen miles eastward from Wigton. It is a burgh royal, having a weekly mercat much frequented, together with some other annual faires. It is situated in a very pleasant place, in a flexure of the river of Dee, more than a large mile from the mouth of that river. It hath an ex-

cellent natural harbour, to which ships of a very great
burthen may at a full sea come, and ly safely from all
stormes, just at the side of the kirk wall. This town is
commonly pronounced Kirkcubree, yea, and commonly
written Kirkudbright; but the true name is Kircudburgh. The Bishop of Edinburgh is patron of the kirk
of Kirkcudburgh, it being a pendicle of New Abbey.
Above the influx of the river of Dee, is the Isle, call'd
of old St Marie's Isle, a priory;[1] and therefore there is
a mistake in John Speed's lesser mapps, (which are the
only mapps I have beside me at present;) for, in his
map of the southern part of Scotland, he places St
Maria on the west side of the mouth of Cree, which
should have been rather placed on the east side of the
mouth of Dee.

12. RERICK. This parish is also called the parish of
Monkton, from the monks that dwelt in the Abbey of
Dundranen; and from the said Abbey, it is also called
the parish of Dundranen. Neer to the Abbey is a rivulet called Greggen, from whence (as some assert) the
abbey, now called and pronounced Dundranen, should
be called Dungreggen. It is reported, (how true I know
not;) that the famous Mr Michael Scot was a monk belonging to this Abbey.[2] This parish of Rerick is bounded,

---

[1] " St Mary's Isle, near Kirkcudbright, in Galloway, was founded,
in the reign of Malcolm IV., or rather David I., by Fergus Lord of
Galloway, and called *Prioratus Sanctæ Mariæ de Trayll.* The
Prior hereof was a Lord and Member of Parliament."—SPOTIS-
WOOD's *Religious Houses.* Chap. II. § 12.

[2] " Dundrenan, an abbey, situate on Solway Frith, about two miles
from Kirkcudbright, in Galloway, was founded by Fergus Lord of
Galloway, in the year 1142. The monks hereof were brought from
Rievall, in England. Sylvanus was the first abbot of this place. He
died at Belleland, 7mo. *Id. Octobris, anno* 1189. The last abbot
hereof was Edward Maxwell, son to John Lord Herries; after
whose death King James VI. annexed this place to his royal-chapel
of Stirling. The Chronicle of Melross is thought to have been writ-

towards the west, with the parish of Kirkcudburgh, (the kirk of Rerick being about four miles distant from the kirk of Kirkcudburgh ;) on the south, it is bounded by the sea ; on the south-east, it is divided from a part of the parish of Cowend by a bay of the river of Orr ; more eastwardly, it is bounded with the parish of Bootle ; and then, from the east, inclining to the north, it is bounded with the parish of Gelston, of which more hereafter in the description of the parish of Kelton. The Bishop of Dunblaine, as Deane of the chapel-royal, is patron of the parish of Rerick, or Dundranen, and hath a part of his revenue paid out of the lands of that Abbacy ; he hath also a bailerie here, heritablie exerc'd by the Earl of Nithisdale, whose jurisdiction reacheth over the whole parish, except one Baronrie called Kirkcastel, belonging to the Laird of Broughton. In this parish of Rerick, there is a good millstone quarrie, on the sea, called Airds-heugh, not far from which is a very safe harbour, called Balcarie, off which lyeth a little island belonging to the Earl of Nithisdale, of about a mile circumference, called the isle of Haston, belonging also to the parish of Rerick, though some say, it belongs to the parish of Bootle, as lying much neerer to it.

13. BOOTLE. This parish-kirk is about nine or ten miles distant from the town of Kirkcudburgh. The Bishop of Edinburgh is patron of this parish also, it being one of the parishes which depend on New Abbey. The kirk was of old called Kirkennen, and was situated

---

ten by an abbot of this monastery. The first part thereof is certainly penned by an Englishman, and is a continuation of Bede's History. The second part appears to have been writ by a Scotsman, familiar and contemporary with our Stuarts. The Oxford edition, published in the year 1684, does not agree with our manuscripts. Alan, Lord of Galloway, sirnamed the Great, Constable of Scotland, was buried in this place, in the year 1233."—SPOTISWOOD's *Religious Houses*, Chap. IX. § 3.

upon the river of Orr, neer the mouth of it ; but for the more conveniency, was translated to the very center of the parish, and called Bootle, because built in the Baronrie so called.   The parish of Bootle is bounded, on the east, by the river of Orr, which divides it from the parishes of Orr and Cowend ; towards the south and west, it is bounded with the parishes of Rerick and Gelston, (of which hereafter in the description of the parish of Kelton ;) towards the north-west, it is bounded with the parish of Kelton ; and towards the north, with the parish of Corsemichael.   In this parish of Bootle, about a mile from the kirk, towards the north, is a well, called the Rumbling Well, frequented by a multitude of sick people, for all sorts of diseases, the first Sunday of May ; lying there the Saturday night, and then drinking of it early in the morning.   There is also another well, about a quarter of a mile distant from the former, towards the east.   This well is made use of by the countrey people, when their cattell are troubled with a disease, called by them the Connoch.   This water they carry in vessells to many parts, and wash their beasts with it, and give it them to drink.   It is too rememb'red, that at both the wells they leave behind them something by way of a thank-offering.   At the first, they leave either money or cloathes ; at the second, they leave the bands and shacles wherewith beasts are usually bound.

14. KELTON.   This parish-kirk is about eight miles distant from the town of Kirkcudburgh.   The Bishop of Edinburgh is also patron hereof, it being one of the parishes depending on New Abbey.   This parish of Kelton is bounded, on the north, with Corsemichael ; toward the north-east, east, and south-east, with the parish of Bootle ; more southerly, with the parish of Rerick ; towards the west, it is bounded with the parish of Kirkcudburgh, as

also by a part of the parishes of Tongueland and Balmaghie, from both which it is separated by the river of Dee. This parish of Kelton hath two other parishes annext thereto, viz. Gelston and Kirkcormock, though both these kirks are ruinous. Gelston, in which the Earl of Galloway pretends an interest, lyes distant from the kirk of Kelton a large mile, towards the south-east. Kirkcormock is only a chapel, and not, as it would seem, a compleat parish, though so ordinarily called. It depends on the Bishop of Edinburgh ; is distant from Kelton about two miles, towards the south-west, the kirk or chapel of Kirkcormock lying upon the very brink of Dee.

15. CORSEMICHAEL. This parish-kirk is twelve miles distant from the town of Kirkcudburgh, keeping the way thereto upon the east side of Dee ; but it is only eight miles the neerest way ; but then you must cross the water of Dee twice, viz. at the boat of Balmaghie, and at the town of Kirkcudburgh. The Bishop of Edinburgh is patron of this kirk also, it being another of the parishes depending on New Abbey. The parish of Corsemichael is bounded, on the east, with the parishes of Kirkpatrick and Orr, from both which it is divided by the river of Orr ; on the south, with the parishes of Bootle and Kelton ; on the west, with the parish of Balmaghie, from which it is separated by the river of Dee ; on the north, it is bounded with the parish of Partan.

16. PARTAN. This parish-kirk (being about two miles, to the northward, distant from the Kirk of Corsemichael) is fourteen miles distant from the town of Kirkcudburgh, keeping the way on the east of Dee ; but it is only ten miles the neerest way, but then the water of Dee must be cross'd twice. There are three pretenders

to the patronage of this kirk ; the Viscount of Kenmuir, the Laird of Partan, and the Laird of Drumrash. Which of them hath the best right, I know not ; but, upon their disagreeing, the Bishop of Galloway is necessitat sometimes to present thereto *jure devoluto.* This parish of Partan is bounded, on the east, with the parishes of Dunscore and Kirkpatrick, from both which it is separated by the water of Orr ; on the south, with the parish of Corsemichael ; on the west, with the parish of Balmaghie, and part of the Kells, from both which it is separated by the river of Dee ; on the north, it is bounded with the parish of Balmaclellan.

These six parishes last described, viz. Kircudburgh, Rerick, Bootle, Kelton, Corsemichael, and Partan, are all lying betwixt the rivers of Orr and Dee.

17. Balmaclellan. This parish-kirk, being about five or six miles to the northward of the Kirk of Partan, will be about twenty miles distant from the town of Kirkcudburgh, by the way on the east side of Dee ; but crossing at the boat of the Rone, viz. at the influx of the river of Dee into the Loch of Kenn, it will be but about fourteen miles distant from Kirkcudburgh. The Bishop of Dumblain is patron of the Kirk of Balmaclellan, as also of the Kirk of the Kells, of which more hereafter. If I mistake not, his right of patronage to these two kirks, is as being Dean to the Chapel-Royal, and as such, hath a right to the Abbacy of Dundranen, and the kirks depending thereon. This parish of Balmaclellan is bounded, on the north, with the parish of Dalry ; on the northeast and east, with the parish of Glencairn, in the shire of Nithisdale, and presbytry of Pinpont ; on the southeast, with the parish of Dunscore, in the said shire of Nithisdale, and presbytry of Dumfreis ; on the south, it is bounded with the parish of Partan ; on the west, with

the parish of the Kells, and separated from it by the river of Kenn.

18. DALRY. This kirk, being about two miles to the northward of Balmaclellan, will be more than twenty miles distant from the town of Kirkcudburgh, going by the way on the east side of Dee; but, crossing the river of Kenn, and thence again crossing at the boat of the Rone, and then again crossing Dee at the town of Kirkcudburgh, it will be but about sixteen miles distant therefrom. The Viscount of Kenmuir is patron of Dalry, and it is, at least should be, a free parsonage. The Kirk of Dalry is seated upon the east brink of the river of Kenn, and there is a very pleasant valley from thence down the river side. About a furlong distant from the east end of the kirk, there is a little town commonly called St John's Clachan, or the Old Clachan, partly belonging to the Earl of Galloway, and partly to the Laird of Earlstoun. This parish is bounded, on the south, with the parish of Balmaclellan; on the west, with the parish of the Kells, from which it is separated by the river of Kenn; on the north, it is separated from the parish of Corsefairn by the said river of Kenn; on the north-east, it is bounded, partly with the parish of Cumlock, in Kyle, and partly with the parish of Sanquhair, in Nithisdale; on the east, it is bounded, partly with the parish of Pinpont, at Polskeoch, and then with the parish of Glencairn, in Nithisdale, from which it is separated by the water of Castlefairne. Severall years since, there was one[1]
who, travelling and trading in England, acquired great riches, and having no children, left a vast summe for maintaining of a free school in the parish of Dalry; but

[1] Where a blank occurs, it will be understood to exist in the original Manuscript.

his money and papers falling into sacrilegious hands, the pious designe of the donor was allmost wholy maid void. However, the affair is not so desperat, but if honest men in that parish would be active in it, they might yet recover a considerable part of it, though far from that which was at first appointed.

19. CORSEFAIRNE. This parish-kirk, being eight miles distant to the northward from Dalry, will be more than twentie-eight miles distant from Kirkcudburgh, going by the way on the east side of Dee; but, crossing the river of Kenn twice, and then crossing Dee at the boat of the Rone, and the boat of Kirkcudburgh, it will be but about twentie-four miles distant therefrom. The Bishop of Galloway is patron of the Kirk of Corsefairne. This parish is in part bounded, on the south, with the parish of Dalry, (and separated therefrom by the river of Kenn,) and in part with the parish of the Kells, being of old a part of the said parish; but now separated therefrom by   Bourn, which emptieth itself into the water of Kenn; on the west, it is bounded with the parish of Monygaffe; on the north-west, with the parish of Dumallington, this parish of Corsefairne, running up as far as Loch Dune; on the north-east and east, with the
In this parish of Corsefairne, there is a considerable water called the Water of Deugh, having its rise in the

and runneth hard by the Kirk of Corsefairne, on the west end thereof, and at length loseth its name, by entering into the river of Kenn, two miles beneath the said Kirk of Corsefairne.

20. KELLS. This parish-kirk will be but about fourteen miles distant from the town of Kirkcudburgh. The Bishop of Dumblain is patron hereof, of which formerly

in the description of the parish of Balmaclellan. The
Kirk of the Kells stands about a short halfe mile on the
west side of the water of Kenn, opposit to the Kirk of
Balmaclellan, which will be more than a mile distant
from the east side of the said river. In this parish, about
a furlong from the west side of the river of Kenn, is a
litle burgh-royal, named New Galloway, or the New
Town, and hath a pretty good mercat every Wednesday,
beside a yearly fair. To the southward of this towne, is
the Castle of Kenmuir, one of the dwelling-houses of the
Viscount of Kenmuir. It is pleasantly situated on a
mount, having a wood of great overgrowne oakes on the
one side, viz. betwixt it and the towne, and on the other
side pleasant meadows, lying on the river of Kenn, which
here begins to run in a deep loch for the space of seaven
or eight miles. But four miles beneath the Kenmuir, at
a point called the boat of the Rone, the river of Dee
meeteth the said loch of Kenn, and from thence to the
sea, the river bears only the name of Dee. This parish
of the Kells is bounded, on the east, with the parishes of
Dalry and Balmaclellan, and a part of Partan, from all
which it is separated by the river of Kenn; upon the
north-east and north, it is bounded with the parish of
Corsefairne, and separated from it by   Bourn,
which empties itselfe into Kenn; on the west, it is bounded with the parish of Monnygaffe, and a point of Girth-
town; and at the boat of the Rone, it is bounded southwardly with the parish of Balmaghie, from which three
parishes it is separated by the river of Dee. This parish
of Kells, excepting about the Newton and the Kenmuir,
is for the most part muirs and mountaines.

These four last parishes above described, viz. Balmaclellan, Dalry, Corsefairne, and the Kells, ly eastward of
the river of Dee; and because the river of Kenn runs

through them, therefore they are commonly called the Glenkennes.

21. BALMAGHIE. This kirk is about seven miles distant from the towne of Kirkcudburgh. The Laird of Balmaghie is patron hereof. The parish of Balmaghie is bounded, on the east, with the parishes of Partan, Corsemichael, and Kelton, from all which it is separated by the river of Dee; on the south, it is bounded with the parish of Tongueland; towards the south-west, it is bounded with the parish of Borgue; westward and northwest, it is bounded with the parish of Girthton; on the north, it is bounded with the parish of Kells, from which it is separated by the river of Dee. In the river of Dee, a little beneath a place called the Granie Foord, lyes an island call'd the Threave, belonging to the said parish of Balmaghie. In this island, the Black Dowglass had a strong house, wherein he sometime dwelt. It is reported, how true I know not, that the peeces of money called Dowglas groats were by him coyned here. As also here it was that he detain'd Sheriff M'Clellan prisoner; and when the king sent him a letter, requiring him to set him at liberty, he, suspecting the purport of the message, took the messenger in, and by discourse entertained him; but in the meantime gave privat orders to hang M'Clellan instantly. At length, the letter being receav'd and opened, and the contents known, he regrated that the letter came no sooner; for the man was just hang'd, which he let the messenger see by opening of a window. The common report also goes in that countrey, that, in this isle of the Threave, the great iron-gun, in the Castle of Edinburgh, called commonly Mount-Megg, was wrought and made; but I am not bound to beleeve it upon their bare report.

22. TONGUELAND. So called from a tongue of land

lying betwixt the river of Dee, and a litle water called
the water of Tarffe, which hath its rise in the same parish. At the meeting of which two waters, there was
the Abbey of Tongueland; the steeple and part of the
wails are yet standing.[1] The Bishop of Galloway is patron hereof, and hath a regality, or at least a baronrie
here; the Viscount of Kenmuir being heritable Bayly
thereof. This kirk is two miles distant from Kirkcudburgh. The parish of Tongueland is bounded, on the
east, with the parishes of Kelton and Kirkcudburgh,
from both which it is separated by the river of Dee;
toward the south and south-west, it is bounded with the
parish of Twynam; more westwardly, it is bounded with
the parish of Borgue; on the west and north-west, with
the parish of Girthton; and on the north, with the parish of Balmaghie.

23. TWYNAM. This kirk is distant two miles northward from Kirkcudburgh. Sir David Dunbar of Baldone
is patron hereof. This parish of Twynam is bounded,
on the east and south, with the parish of Kirkcudburgh,
from which it is divided by the river of Dee; on the
west, with the parish of Borgue. The parish of Twynam
hath another kirk annexed thereto, though altogether
ruinous, called Kirkchrist, lying upon the west side of
the river of Dee, not far from the brink thereof, just opposit to the town of Kirkcudburgh.

[1] " Tungland, in Galloway, was founded by Fergus, Lord of Galloway, in the twelfth century. Alexander, Abbot of Tungland, is
one of the subscribers to Ragman's Roll, in the year 1296. Lesly
tells us a very merry story of another Abbot of this place, p. 331. *ad
annum* 1507, who, undertaking to be in France before the king's
ambassadors who were going thither, by flying in the air, and accordingly taking his flight from the walls of the Castle of Stirling, met
with a reward suitable to the nature of the undertaking, by falling
and breaking his thigh-bones. A like story is related by Radulphus
Hygdenus, lib. vi. p. 284, *ad annum Christi* 1065."—SPOTISWOOD'S
Religious Houses, Chap. V. § 5.

24. BORGUE. This parish-kirk is three miles westward distant from Kirkcudburgh. The Bishop of Galloway is patron of this parish. On the east, it is bounded
with the parish of Kirkcudburgh, from which it is divided
by the river Deè; on the south, it is bounded by the sea;
on the west and part of the north, by the parish of Girthton; on the north also, in part, and wholy on the north-
east, by the parish of Twynam. This parish of Borgue
hath two other parishes annexed thereto; the one called
Kirkanders, and the other Senick, whereof the Bishop of
Galloway is also patron. This parish of Borgue, with
the other two parishes annext thereto, is about four miles
in length, and for the most part three in breadth, except
towards the foot thereof, towards the sea-side, where it
will be four miles broad. The minister hereof is one of
the members of the Chapter, and of old was Precentor.
This parish abounds with plenty of corne, wherewith it
furnishes many other places in the Stewartrie, supplying
them both with meal and malt. In the middle of this parish, there is a good strong house, called the Castle of
Plunton-Lennox, possess'd of a long time by the name of
Lennox, till of late, when it came into the possession of
Richard Murray of Broughton, whose lady is one of that
name and family. In the parish of Sennick, there is a
very famous and large harbour, called the bay of Bal-
mangand; it is one of the best harbours in the west of
Scotland; for there ships of all sizes are secure, blow the
wind which way it will. Adjacent to this bay, is a promontory called the Mickle Ross, wherein is to be seen
the ruines of an old castle, where, in times past, some of
the inhabitants have digg'd up silver-plate, as I am informed; as also therein have found certain peeces of silver, with a strange and uncouth impression thereon, re-

sembling the old Pictish coine. Half a mile from the Ross, is the famous Well of Kissickton, medicinal, as it is reported, for all sorts of diseases; the people hereabouts flocking to it in the summer-time. In the kirkyard of Kirkanders, upon the ninth day of August, there is a fair kept, called St Lawrence Fair, where all sorts of merchant-wares are to be sold; but the fair lasts only three or four houres, and then the people, who flock hither in great companies, drink and debauch, and commonly great lewdness is committed here at this fair. A little above Roberton, within halfe a mile of the Kirk of Kirkanders, is to be seen the ruines of an old town call'd Rattra, wherein, as the present inhabitants thereabouts say, was of old kept a weekly market; but the town is long since demolished, and neer the ruines thereof is now a little village, which yet retaines the name of the old town. Upon the coast of this parish are many sorts of white fish taken; one kind whereof is called by the inhabitants Greyheads, which are a very fine firm fish, big like haddocks, some greater, some lesser.

25. GIRTHTON. This parish-kirk is about five miles to the westward of Kirkcudburgh. The Bishop of Galloway is patron hereof. This parish of Girthton is bounded, on the east, with the parishes of Balmaghie and Borgue; on the south, with the sea; on the west, it is divided from the parish of Anwoth by the water of Fleet, (Speed calls it Flint,) that hath its rise from the great mountain of Cairnsmuir, lying to the north-west; on the north-west, it joynes with the parish of Kirkmabreck; on the north, it is bounded with the parish of Monnygaffe; and on the north-east, with the parish of the Kells, from which it is separated by the river of Dee. About two miles from the Kirk of Girthton, in the road way betwixt Dumfreise and Wigton, at a place called the

Gatehouse of Fleet, there is a market for good fat kine
kept on the Friday, after the first Thursday, which is
after the first Monday of November, and so every Friday
thereafter till Christmas.   This market being rul'd by
the dyets of the nolt-market of Wigton, of which more
hereafter in the description of that town and parish.

26. ANWOTH.   This parish-kirk is near seaven miles
distant from the town of Kircudburgh westward, just in
the way betwixt Kirkcudburgh and Wigton.   Sir Godfrey M'Culloch of Myrton, as Laird of Cardiness, is patron hereof. It is separated, on the east, from the parish
of Girthton by the water of Fleet; on the south, it is
bounded on the sea ; on the west, it is divided from the
parish of Kirkmabreck by a rivulet called Skairsbourn,
which, having its rise from Cairnsmuir, and the adjacent
northern mountains, will, even in the summer time, and
in a moment almost, by reason of the mists and vapours
in those hills, be so great, that it will be hardly foordable, which occasioned the proverb of *Skairsbourn's warning*, applicable to any trouble that comes suddenly and
unexpectedly. This sudden inundation proceeds, as said
is, from the mists and vapours on Cairnsmuir ; hence the
common people say, *When that Cairnsmuir hath a hat,
Palnure* (of which more hereafter in the description of
the river of Cree) *and Skairsbourn laugh at that.* On
the north, the parish of Anwoth is bounded with the parishes of Kirkmabreck and Girthton.

27. KIRKMABRECK; so called from some Saint or
other, whose name was, they say, M'Breck, a part of
whose statue in wood, was, about thirty years since, in
an old chapel at the Ferrietown, distant about
to the   of the Kirk of Kirkmabreck ; which
kirk, about thirty years since, was taken down and left
desolate, and the parish-kirk was then built at the said

chapel; and therefore the parish is sometimes also called the Ferrietown, which Ferrietown is a little clachan upon the east side of the river of Cree, where there us'd to be a boat for the ferrying of passengers over the water of Cree in their passage to Wigton, which is just opposit thereto, and in view thereof, though three or four miles distant. This Kirk of Ferrietown is twelve miles distant from Kirkcudburgh westward. The Laird of Rusco is patron hereof. It hath another parish annexed thereto, called Kirkdale or Kirdale, being distant from the old Kirk of Kirkmabreck about a mile towards the   , and is a pendicle of the Abbacy of Dundranen; the kirk is wholly ruinous. About a furlong from the Kirk of Kirkdale, towards the south-east, there is a cairn, or great heap of small hand-stones, with five or six high stones erected; besides which high stones, the smaller ones being removed by the countrey people for building of their corne-dikes, there were five or six tombs discovered, made of thin whin-stones. In Camerot-muir, in the said parish of Kirkdale, about a mile from the said kirk northward, there is a stone four or five feet in diameter, called the Penny-stone, under which money is fancied to be. This stone hath upon it the resemblance of that draught which is commonly called the walls of Troy. The manse belonging to the minister of Kirkmabreck, or Ferrietown, is called the Halfe-mark, and will be a mile distant from the Ferrietown, southwardly upon the bank of the river of Cree. It is a very pleasant place, and the minister hath the benefit of a salmon-fishing there. This manse, called the Halfe-mark, is distant to the westward about halfe a mile from the old Kirk of Kirkmabreck, neer to which old Kirk of Kirkmabreck, there is a well, which, as I am informed, proceeds from vitriol. This parish of Kirkmabreck, with the annext parish of

Kirkdale, is bounded, on the east, with the parish of Anwoth, and separated from it by the little rivulet called Scairsbourn, which empties itselfe into the sea; on the south, it is bounded with the sea; on the east, with the river of Cree, which here, at an high water, will be three or four miles broad, though, at low water, it is contain'd in a narrow chanel; it divides betwixt Kirkmabreck and the Shire of Wigton; on the north, it is bounded with the parish of Monnygaffe, and divided in part therefrom by the Graddock Bourn, which hath its rise in the mountain of Cairnsmuir, and running westward, empties itselfe into the river of Cree.

These seaven parishes last described, (viz. Balmaghie, Tongueland, Twynam, Borgue, Girthton, Anwoth, and Kirkmabreck, as also Monygaffe, of which hereafter,) ly betwixt the rivers of Dee and Cree.

The seaventeen parishes last described, viz. Kirkcudburgh, Rerick, Bootle, Kelton, Corsemichael, Partan, Balmaclellan, Dalry, Corsefairn, Kells, Balmaghie, Tongueland, Twynam, Borgue, Girthton, Anwoth, and Kirkmabreck, make up the Presbytry of Kirkcudburgh, one of the three Presbyteries within the Dioces of Galloway. Kirkcudburgh is the ordinary seat of that Presbytrie, where the members of the Presbytrie meet most commonly upon the first Tuesday of every month, for exercing of church discipline, and other ecclesiastical affaires incumbent on them.

The Commissary of Kirkcudburgh also hath jurisdiction over these seaventeen parishes, in reference to causes consistorial. He derives his authority from the Bishop of Galloway, and holds his courts ordinarly at the town of Kirkcudburgh on every Fryday, except in times of vacance.

28. MONNYGAFFE; so called, as I suppose, qu. Mun-

nach's Gulfe, from the river of Munnach in this parish, which, after many windings and turnings, empties itselfe into the river of Cree. The parish-kirk of Monnygaffe, lying six miles to the north-west of the Ferrietown, or Kirkmabreck, is eighteen miles distant from the town of Kirkcudburgh, and six miles to the northward of Wigton. The Bishop of Galloway is patron hereof. This parish is bounded, on the east, with the water of Dee, by which it is separated from the parishes of Corsefairne and the Kells; towards the south-east, and more southwardly, it is bounded with the parish of Girthton; on the south, with the parish of Kirkmabreck, from which it is in part separated by the Graddock Bourne; on the west, it is bounded with the parish of Pennygham, in the Shire of Wigton, from which it is separated by the river of Cree; on the north-west, it is bounded with the parish of Cammonel, in Carrick, from which it is also separated by the river of Cree; more northward, it is bounded partly with the parish of Barr, in Carrick, and partly with the parish of Dumallington, in Kyle; so that this parish of Monnygaffe is exactly lying betwixt the rivers of Dee and Cree; and though lying within the bounds of the Stewartrie of Kirkcudburgh, and subject to the Stewart thereof, of which more hereafter, yet it belongs both to the Presbytry and Commissariot of Wigton, by reason that it is eighteen miles distant from the town of Kirkcudburgh, and the way not very good ether, when as it is but six miles from Wigton, and that excellent good way, both winter and summer. And it is also most fit it should belong to the Commissariot of Wigton, because having a weekly mercat in it, which is for the most part supplied by people dwelling in that Commissariot, those people who supply that mercat with meal, malt, &c. would be put to excessive trouble, should they be necessitat to pursue their debitors, which often happens, before the Stewart, for small summs at so great a distance.

This parish of Monnygaffe is a very large one, being at least sixteen miles in length, and eight miles in breadth ; the greatest part whereof consists of great hills, mountains, rocks, and moors. It hath in it a little town, or burgh of baronrie, depending upon the Laird of Larg, situated upon the east side of the river of Cree, neer the brink thereof. It hath a very considerable market every Saturday, frequented by the moormen of Carrick, Monnygaffe, and other moor places, who buy there great quantities of meal and malt, brought thither out of the parishes of Whitherne, Glaston, Sorbie, Mochrum, Kirkinner, &c. of which places we shall have occasion to speake, when we come to the Shire. The Kirk of Monnygaffe is divided from the town by a rivulet called Pinkill Bourn, which is sometimes so great, that the people, in repairing to the church, are necessitat to go almost a mile about, crossing at a bridge built over the said rivulet, a short halfe mile above the town. The farthest part of this parish is at least twelve miles distant northward from the parish-kirk, and the way excessively bad ; and therefore it hath been many times wisht that the parish were disjoyn'd, and made two parishes, and another kirk built at a place, called the House of the Hill, some six miles northward, in the highway betwixt Wigton and Air. The inhabitants of that upper part of the parish would be content to contribute something to that effect. It hath been endeavoured to get a kirk erected there ; but as yet that affair hath been unsuccessfull ; and for any thing I know, will continue so to be, unless people concerned therein will learn to be more religious, which I fear, will not be in hast.

Principal edifices in this parish, are (1.) Gairlies, the ancient residence of the Lairds of Gairlies, before that family was nobilitated; it doth yet furnish a title to the Earl of Galloway his eldest son, who is Lord Gairlies. This house, being about a mile to the northward of the kirk and town, stands in the midst of a very fine oak wood, pertaining to the said Earl, who also hath another excellent oak wood in this parish, lying upon the water of Cree, two miles above the kirk and town. This wood will be two or three miles in length, and hath good timber in it, from whence the greatest part of the Shire of Wigton furnish timber for building of houses and other uses. The Earl of Galloway's lands in this parish being very considerable here, are, as I have been informed, erected into a Stewartrie, and the said Earl is heritable Stewart thereof. (2.) Larg, appertaining to M'Kie of Larg, a very ancient name and family in this countrey. Hereabout is a well, called the Gout-well of Larg, of which they tell this story, how that a piper stole away the offering left at this well, (these offerings are some inconsiderable thing, which the countrey people use to leave at wells, when they come to make use of them towards any cure;) but when he was drinking of ale, which he intended to pay with the money he had taken away, the gout, as they say, seiz'd on him, of which he could not be cur'd but at that well, having first restor'd to it the money he had formerly taken away. (3.) Macchirmore, or the Head of the Macchirs, (of which word more hereafter,) for indeed there is not much white ground above it, pertaining to Dunbar of Macchirmore. It is situated upon the east side of the river of Cree, one mile distant to the south from the town of Monnygaffe; and here is the first foord of the water of Cree, except that betwixt Kirkmabreck and Wigton, of which more hereafter. This

foord is five miles or thereby in *rectâ lineâ* to the northward distant from Wigton.   In the moors of this parish
of Monnygaffe, not many years since, at a place called
La Spraig, not far from the water of Munnach, but sixteen miles distant from the sea, there fell a shower of
herring, which were seen by creditable persons who related the story to me. Some of the said herring were, as
I am informed, taken to the Earl of Galloway's house,
and shown to him.[1]

These twentie-eight parishes, viz. 1. Traqueer; 2. New
Abbey; 3. Kirkbeen; 4. Cowend, including also Southwick; 5. Orr; 6. Kirkpatrick Durham; 7. Kirkpatrick
Iron Gray; 8. Terregles; 9. Lochruiton; 10. Kirkgunnion; 11. Kirkcudburgh, including also Galtway and
Dunrod; 12. Rerick, or Monkton, or Dundranen; 13.
Bootle; 14. Kelton, including also Gelston and Kirkcormock; 15. Corsemichael; 16. Partan; 17. Balmaclellan; 18. Dalry; 19. Corsefairne; 20. Kells; 21.
Balmaghie; 22. Tongueland; 23. Twynam, including
also Kirkchrist; 24. Borgue, including also Kirkanders
and Sennick; 25. Girthton; 26. Anwoth; 27. Kirkmabreck, or Ferriton, including also Kirkdale; 28. Monnygaffe, are lyable to the Stewart of Kirkcudburgh, which
office belongs heritably to the Earl of Nithisdale, and is
at present, by reason of the minority of the present Earl,
exerc'd by Sir Robert Grierson of Lag, who keeps his
head court at the town· of Kirkcudburgh, and his ordinary courts there also, either by himselfe or his deputs,
for administrating of justice on every   , except
in vacation time.   For the benefit of the ten kirks beneath Orr, he hath also a deput who keeps courts at
Lochruiton.

[1] Appendix, No. IV.

The Stewartry of Kirkcudburgh, (although exceeding the Shire of Wigton both in bounds and valuation,) sends only one Commissioner to the Parliament, or Convention of Estates. But it is now high time, I suppose, that we crosse the river of Cree, and go to the Shire of Wigton.

SHIRE OF WIGTON.

THE Shire of Wigton is bounded, on the east, with the Stewartry of Kirkcudburgh, and parted from it by the river of Cree; on the south-west and north-west, it is environed with the sea; on the north, it is bounded, partly with Carrick, and partly with the Stewartry of Kirkcudburgh, viz. at or toward the head of Monnygaffe, being parted therefrom also with the river of Cree, which towards the head bends something to the westward.

The Shire of Wigton extends in length, viz. from the town of Wigton, to the point of the Mule of Galloway, twentie-eight or thirty miles; or rather, counting from the brink of the river of Cree, at the Ferrietown, it will be about thirty-four miles in length. As for the breadth of it, from the Isle of Whithern to the borders of Carrick, it will be more than twentie miles, although, in some other parts of the Shire, the breadth will not be so much.[1]

The Shire of Wigton contains in it sixteen principal parishes, viz.

[1] Appendix, No. V.

C

1. WIGTON. The Earl of Galloway is patron. It is
a Parsonage, though but a small one. It is bounded, on
the south, with the parish of Kirkinner, and separated
from it by the river of Blaidnoch; on the west, north,
and east, it is surrounded with the parish of Penygham,
and separated therefrom, on the north and east, with a
rivulet, called the Bishop Bourn, which empties itself
into the river of Blaidnoch, or Cree, on the sands beneath
Wigton. This parish hath in it a burgh-royal, called
also Wigton, which town, as the inhabitants say, of old
stood more than a mile eastward; but that place is now
covered with the sea every tide. However, this is certain, that of old it was called Epiack or Epiacte. A friend
of mine conjectures, and doubtless it is but a conjecture,
that it was so called from Danewort or Dwarfe Elder,
call'd also Chamiacte; however, sure I am this herb or
shrub, call it as you please, grows here in great abundance, and overspreads much of their beir-land, on the
south-east part of the towne. And since we are speaking
of an herb, I think fit to add, that Henbane grows also
very plentifully in the towne through the streets, and
upon every dunghill there. This town is the head burgh
of the Shire, although it stands at the eastmost end thereof. Ships of two hundred tun may come neer to it at a
spring-tide, with a good pilot; but yet it hath but little
trading by sea. They choose annually a Provest, two
Bayliffs, and a Treasurer, with severall other Counsel-
lours. Fryday is the day of their town-court. It is a
town of small tradeing; their market-day is Monday;
but is not frequented. However, they have four yearly
faires which are considerable; the first is call'd the Palm
Fair, which beginns the fifth Monday in Lent, and lasts
two days; the second, Midsummer Fair, or rather St
Alban's Fair; for, on the seventeenth day of June, St

Alban's day, if it fall upon a Friday, or if not then the next
Fryday thereafter, they have a market for horses and
young phillies, which the Borderers from Annandale, and
places thereabout, (the stile the countrey calls them by,
is Johnnies,) come and buy in great numbers. The Monday and Tuesday thereafter, they have a fair frequented
by merchants from Edinburgh, Glasgow, Air, and other
places, who here buy great quantities of raw broad cloath,
and transport part of it over seas, and part of it they dy
at home, and sell for many uses. The third and greatest fair is call'd Lambmas Fair, which is allways just six
weeks distant from the former ; for, on the Fryday before the first Monday of August, they have another market for horses, much frequented by the forsaid Johnnies ;
and then, on the next Monday and Tuesday, viz. the first
Monday and Tuesday of August, they have the cloath
fair, which is more frequented than the Midsummer fair,
both by buyers and sellers, because the countrey people
have then had a longer time to work, and make their
webbs ready, which they could not get done at the former fair. This fair is so considerable, that, as I have
been informed, no fewer than eighteen score of packs of
cloath have been sold thereat. The fourth is their Martimas Fair, which beginns allways upon the first Monday
of November, and lasts two days. The next Thursday
after this first Monday of November, and so every Thursday thereafter till Christmas, they have a market for fat
kine ; this market is frequented by butchers and others
from Dumfries, and other places thereabout, for four or
five market-days only ; for in that time all the fattest and
best kine are sold and gon.

This town of Wigton is indifferently well built, with
pretty good houses three story high toward the street,
especialy on the north side. The street is very broad

and large. The parish-kirk stands a little without the east port. The Tolbooth, standing neer the middle of the town, is lately beautify'd with a Pyramis, erected upon a square platforme, upon the top of the steeple, set round with pylasters, which adds a fine ornament to the town. This town stands very pleasantly, being built upon a large and fruitfull hill, of an easie ascent every way. On the south-east of this town, there was long since a Friarie; but the very ruines thereof are now allmost ruined.[1] The greatest quantity of agrimony that I ever saw in one place, grows about this Friarie. In this town of Wigton, about seaven or eight years since, there was a woman call'd Margaret Blain, yet living there, wife to John M'Craccan, a taylor, who is also yet living, who was brought to bed of three children, who were orderly baptized, having a quarter of a year or thereabout before that miscarried of another.

In the parish, there are no considerable edifices except one, viz. Torhouse, situated on the north side of the river of Blaidnoch, and belongs to George M'Culloch of Torhouse, not far from whose house, in the highway betwixt Wigton and Portpatrick, about three miles westward of Wigton, is a plaine call'd the Moor, or Standing Stones of Torhouse, in which there is a monnment of three large whin-stones, call'd King Galdus's tomb, surrounded, at about twenty foot distance, with nineteen considerable great stones, (but none of them so great as the three first mentioned,) erected in a circumference. In this Moor, and not far from the tomb, are great heaps of small hand-stones, which the countrey people call Cairnes, suppos'd

---

[1] " Wigton, in the shire of the same name. The Convent at this place was founded in the year 1267, by Dervorgilla, daughter to Alan Lord of Galloway, and mother to John Baliol, King of Scotland."— SPOTISWOOD's *Religious Houses*, Chap. XV. § 10.

by them to be the buriall places of the common souldiers.
As also at severall places distant from the monument, are
here and there great single stones erected, which are also
supposed to be the buriall places of his commanders and
men of note. But herein I determine nothing, only I think
fit to add, that, at severall places in this countrey, there
are many great heaps of hand-stones, call'd Cairnes ; and
those heaps, or Cairnes, of stones are very seldom single,
but many times there are two of them, and sometimes
more, not far distant from each other. This place is the
ordinary rendezvouse of the militia-troop, which belongs
to the Shire: This parish of Wigton is allmost equal in
breadth and length, being about three miles and an halfe
extent every way.

2. PENYGHAM. The Earl of Galloway is patron of
this parish-kirk, which is about four miles northward
distant from the town of Wigton ; and therefore here
again we may take notice of a mistake in Speed's map,
which placeth Penygham neer the sea beyond Whithern,
to the southward of Wigton about nine or ten miles.
This parish of Penygham is bounded, on the east, partly
with the parish of Kirkmabreck, and partly with the parish of Monnygaffe, from both which it is parted by the
river of Cree ; on the north, it is bounded also with the
parish of Monnygaffe, and parted also from it by the river
of Cree ; on the north-west, it is bounded with the parish
of Cammonnel, in Carrick ; on the west, with the parish
of Kirkcowan, and divided therefrom by the river of
Blaidnoch ; on the south-west, it runns out in a point,
which point is on the east bounded with the parish of
Wigton, and on the south part of it, parted from the parish of Kirkinner by the river of Blaidnoch. The parish
of Penygham is bounded, on the south and south-east,
with the parish of Wigton, and parted from it by a
rivulet, called the Bishop's Bourn. This parish of Peny-

gham is in length twelve miles, in breadth more than
four; the farthest part of it is nine miles distant from
the parish-church. It was of old the residence of the
Bishop of Galloway, who hath yet a jurisdiction here,
call'd the Lordship of Penygham, comprehending such
lands, as in this parish hold of the Bishop of Galloway.
The Earl of Cassillis is Heritable Bayly of this jurisdiction. There is at present a bell at the Church of Penygham, with this inscription in Saxon letters, *Campana
Sancti Niniani de Penygham, M.*, dedicat, as it seems,
to Saint Ninian, in the thousand year after the birth of
Christ. There is a ruinous chapel in this parish, call'd
the Chapel of the Cruives, situated on the west side of
the river of Cree, four miles distant from the parish-kirk,
which was long since appropriated for divine service, but
now ruinous.

The principal edefices in this parish, are, 1. The
Clary, the Earl of Galloway his winter residence, distant a short halfe mile from the kirk, in the way to
Wigton. 2. Castle Stewart, distant about four miles
from the kirk, towards the north, in the way to the town
of Air. It is the residence of William Stewart, of Castle
Stewart, youngest brother to the present Earl of Galloway, belonging to him in right of his lady, grandchild to
that expert and valiant collonell, William Stewart of
Castle Stewart, a valiant and fortunat souldier in the
German warrs, under the command of Gustavus Adolphus, King of Sweden. Of this Collonell Stewart's lady,
grandmother to the present Lady Castle Stewart, I have
heard a strange passage, which I think fit to insert, viz.
The said lady, before her husband went to the wars, one
day combing her hair in the sun, her sight wholy departed from her; after which her husband betook himselfe to the warrs in Germany, and was there advanc'd to
be a collonell, his lady in the meantime remaining at

home blind ; at length she resolves, blind as she was, to visit her husband, and taking a servant with her, took shipping for Holland, from whence, after a tedious journey, she came to Germany ; and enquiring for the army, and among them for the Scots regiments, met there with her husband, who own'd and receaved her. The lady being there, and, some say seaven yeares after her blindness, combing her hair, some report in the sun also, yea, and the same day of the month that it departed from her, her sight was restored as perfectly as at the first. The truth of this story, in all its circumstances, I do not assert, but only relate it as I heard it ; however, this is most certain, that, by her being with him in Germany, she so manag'd what was acquir'd there, that with it he purchast a fair estate in Galloway, possess'd at present by her grandchild. And since I have related a passage (as I have heard it) of the wife, I'le add a passage of the husband, of the which a very judicious person assures me he was an eye witness, viz. The said Collonell Stewart being at home here in Galloway, was affected with a palsie for the space of about a year and an halfe, which affected the one side from head to foot, (occasioned perhaps through loss of blood in the wars,) and yet he fell into a most violent feaver, which affected the other side only ; he recovered of the feaver in a month's time or thereby, and liv'd neer two years after that ; but the palsie continued till his dying day. The minister of Penygham assures me also, that there is a gentlewoman at present living in his parish, that for a long time hath had the palsie on the one side, and lately had a violent feaver on the other side ; out of which feaver she is now recovered, her palsie remaining. 3. Glasnick, the residence of James Gordon, younger of Craichlaw. This house stands on the east side of the river of Blaidnoch ; and is distant about three miles from the parish-kirk, to the westward. 4. The

Grainge, belonging heritably to John Gordon of Grainge. This house stands upon the north and east side of the river Blaidnoch, neer a flexure of the said river ; and is distant about three miles from the parish-kirk, to the south-westward.

These two parishes of Wigton and Penygliam, are almost environed with the rivers of Cree and Blaidnoch ; both which rivers, after severall windings and turnings, meet together a litle below Wigton, and there empty themselves into the sea.

3. KIRKINNER. This parish-kirk is about two miles distant from Wigton, southward. The patronage of this parish of Kirkinner is controverted. The Laird of Barn-barroch claimes it by vertue of a gift from King James the Sixth, to his great grandfather, Sir Patrick Vans, who was also one of the Lords of the Session, and was sent to Denmark to wait upon Queen Anne. The Sub-dean of his Majestie's Chapel-Royall claimes it as titular of the teinds of the said parish. This parish of Kirkinner hath another little parish, called Long Castle, annext thereto, where was a little church for divine service, about two miles and an halfe distant from the Kirk of Kirkinner, to the westward, in the way to the Kirk of Mochrum ; but now the said Kirk of Longcastle is ruinous. In this parish of Longcastle, at a place called Cairnfield, there is a monument, almost like that call'd Galdus Tomb, in the parish of Wigton ; but it consists not of so good stones, nor yet placed in so good order. The parish of Kirkinner, with Longcastle annexed thereto, is bounded on the east with the parish of Kirkmabreck, and separated therefrom by the river of Cree, and the large sands of Kirkinner ; on the south it is partly bounded with the parish of Sorbie, and partly with the parish of Glasserton ; from which last parish it is in part separated by the Loch of

Longcastle, called on the other side the Loch of Ravin-
ston; on the west it is bounded with the parish of Mochrum; on the north-west, with the parish of Kirkcowan;
on the north, it is in a little part only bounded with the
parish of Penygham; and for the other parts, bounded
with the parish of Wigton; from both which parishes it
is separated by the River of Blaidnoch.   In this parish
of Kirkinner, Sir David Dunbar of Baldone hath a park,
about two miles and an halfe in length, and a mile and an
halfe in breadth; the greatest part whereof is rich and
deep valley ground, and yeelds excellent grass; upon the
north side, it is separated from the parish of Wigton, by
the river of Blaidnoch; on the east side, it lyes open to
the sea sands, which, at low water, will be about two
miles betwixt the bank of the said park, and the chanel
of the River of Cree, which divides it from the parish of
Kirkmabreck, in the Stewartry.   This park can keep in
it, winter and summer, about a thousand bestiall, part
whereof he buys from the countrey, and grazeth there
all winter, other part whereof is of his owne breed; for he
hath neer two hundred milch kine, which for the most
have calves yearly.   He buys also in the summer time
from the countrey many bestiall, oxen for the most part,
which he keeps till August or September; so that yearly he ether sells at home to drovers, or sends to Saint
Faiths, Satch, and other faires in England, about eighteen
or twentie score of bestiall.   Those of his owne breed, at
four year old, are very large; yea, so large, that in August or September, 1682, nine and fifty of that sort,
which would have yeelded betwixt five and six pound
sterling the peece, were seized upon in England for Irish
cattell; and because the person to whom they were entrusted, had not witnesses there ready at the precise
hour, to swear that they were seen calved in Scotland,

(though the witness offered to depone that he liv'd in
Scotland, within a mile of the park where they were
calved and bred,) they were, by the sentence of Sir J.
L., and some others, who knew well enough that they
were bred in Scotland, knockt on the head and kill'd;
which was, to say no more, very hard measure, and an
act unworthy of persons of that quality and station, who
ordered it to be done.

On the bank of this park, that lyes opposit to the sea,
if there be in the winter time any high tides and storms
from the south-east, the sea casts in innumerable and incredible quantities of cockle-shells, which the whole shire
makes use of for lime, and it is the onely lime which this
countrey affoords. The way of making it is thus: Upon
an even area, (the circumference they make less or more,
according to the quantity of the shells they intend to
burne,) they set erected peits, upon which they put a
layer of shells, a foot thick or more, and then upon them
again lay peits, though not erected as at first, and then
another layer of shells, and so, *stratum super stratum*,
till they bring it to an head like a pyramis; but as they
put on these layers just in the center, they make a tunnel of peits, like a chimney, hollow in the middest, reaching from the bottom to the top, (just almost as Evelyn
describes the making of charcoal;) this done, they take
a pan full of burning peits, and put them down into this
tunnel, or chimney, and so close up all with shells. This
fire kindles the whole kilne, and in twentie-four hours
space, or thereby, will so burn the shells that they will
run together in an hard masse; after this, they let it cool
a little, and then with an iron spade they bring it down
by degrees, and sprinkling water thereon, with a beater
they beat it, (or *berry* it, for that's their terme; this
word they also use for threshing, and so call the thresher

of their corne, the *berrier*,) and then put it so beaten into little heaps, which they press together with the broad side of their spade, after which, in a short time, it will dissolve (they call it melting) into a small white powder, and it is excellent lime. I have heard good masons say, that, as it is whiter, so also it binds stones together surer and better than stone-lime itselfe.

When the tide is ebbing from these banks, severall of the countrey people, in summer and harvest-time, use to go a-fishing with the halfe net, the forme and use whereof take as follows: They take four peeces of oake, alder, or willow, about three inches diameter, which they contrive almost into the forme of a semicircle, about fourteen or fifteen foot diameter at the points, and about five or six foot diameter the other way, with a balk athwart to keep all firme. These four peeces of timber they nail fast together, putting also three or four lesser crosse peeces of timber to make it more firme. To this they fasten a net much wider than the stales, (for so they term the frame of timber.) With this, at the ebbing of the tide, they go into the water till it comes up to their breast, and sometimes to their shoulders, and turning their faces towards the streame, put the stale points to the ground, so that the net being large and wide, is carried by the streame on ether side ; from each corner of the net they have a warning-string comeing, which they hold in their hand, which gives them warning when the least fish comes in the net, and then presently they pull the stale-points from the ground, which are instantly wafted to the top of the water, and so catch the fish. By this meanes they catch fleuks, solefleuks, turbets, and severall other fish, yea, and oftentimes many salmon too ; and thus they continue till low water, moving allways farther and farther, as the water ebbs ; and

then when the tide turns, they turn about to the stream,
and do as formerly.

The principall edifices in this parish of Kirkinner, are,
1. Barnbarroch, the residence of John Vans of Barnbarroch; it lys about a mile from the kirk to the westward.
2. Baldone, the residence of Sir David Dunbar of Baldone, Knight-Baronet; it is seated in the Park, and will
be about a short mile from the kirk to the northward,
towards the towne of Wigton. The whole parish of
Kirkinner, the annext parish of Longcastle being included, is about four miles and an halfe in length, and
about as much in breadth; the farthest part from the
kirk will be about three miles and an halfe. This parish
of Kirkinner, (viz. about the kirk, there being neer halfe
a score of excellent spring-wells hard by it, and in the
Park,) is accounted the best place hereabout for fowling
in the winter time, having then in it great abundance of
wild geese, wild ducks, teales, woodcocks, &c.

4. Sorbie. The Bishop of Galloway is patron of this
parish-kirk. The distance of which from the town of Wigton, is about five short miles to the southward, the Kirk of
Kirkinner being in the highway (and almost of an equall
distance) betwixt them. This parish of Sorbie hath two
other little parishes united to it, viz. Kirkmadroyn, lying
on the sea eastward, but the kirk is ruinous; and Crugleton, lying also towards the sea more southwards; the
kirk thereof is also ruinous. The parish of Sorbie, the
said two annex'd kirks being included, is bounded, on
the north, with Kirkinner; on the east, south-east, and
south, with the sea; on the south and south-west, with
the parish of Whitherne; on the west, with the parish
of Glasserton. The parish of Sorbie, with the two annext parishes, will be in length scarce four miles, and
in breadth about three miles, the farthest part whereof

will not be much above two miles distant from the parish-kirk.

There is only one principal edifice in this parish, called the Place of Sorbie, seated about halfe a mile from the kirk to the east thereof; it is a very good house; 'twas built by the Laird of Sorbie, whose name was then Hannay, a name very common in Galloway, but not any man now of note of that name in this countrey. This house now appertaines to the Earl of Galloway. In the parish of Kirkmadroyne, there is a place called Enderwell, to which ships may have recourse in time of storme. In the parish of Crugleton, there was long since, upon an high cliffe on the sea-side, a very strong house, called the Castle of Crugleton, but it is now wholy demolish'd and ruinous; it appertaines to Sir Andrew Agnew of Lochnaw. In this parish of Crugleton, there is also a bay, call'd Polton, whereat, in the months of July, August, and September, there uses to be a herring-fishing; in some years, they are so plentifull, that they are sold for five groats, or two shillings the maze, (each maze contains five hundred, at sixscore to the hundred,) and sometimes cheaper. But it is only in some yeares that this plenty happens; and I have heard some people say, that it seldome comes to pass that the sea and land are plentifull in one and the same year.

5. WHITHERNE. This kirk lyes about eight miles from Wigton southward, and about three miles from the Kirk of Sorbie. The Bishop of Galloway is patron hereof. This parish is bounded, on the south, with the sea; on the west, with the parish of Glasserton; on the north, north-east, and east, with the parish of Sorbie; the Baronrie of Broughton, in this parish of Whitherne, running out in a point betwixt the two Kirks of Sorbie and Crugleton. The parish of Whitherne is in length about four

miles and an halfe, in breadth not so much ; the farthest part will be but two miles from the kirk. In this parish, there is a burgh-royal, call'd Whitherne, (from whence the parish hath its name) Candida Casa, or White-herne ; Herne signifying a cottage in the Saxon language. They choose annualy a Provest, two Baylies, and a Treasurer, (but there is little use for him,) with severall other Councellours. Their market-day is Saturday ; but it is not at all frequented. It is a towne of little or no trade at present, although of old it was a town of great trade and resort. They have a very advantageous port belonging to them, call'd the Isle of Whitherne, two miles distant from the town southwards, in which ships of a great burthen may be in safety in time of any storme.

There was in this town a famous Priory,[1] and a stately church, founded by St Ninian, and dedicated by him to his unckle St Martin, Bishop of Tours, in France, as I have heard it reported. Sure I am there is a little hand-bell in this church, which, in Saxon letters, tells it belongs to Saint Martin's church. The steeple and body of the church is yet standing, together with some of the walls of the precincts. The Isles, Crosse-church, and severall other houses belonging thereto, are fallen ; but

---

[1] " Whitehorn, or Candida Casa, a Bishop's seat in Galloway. Fergus, Lord of Galloway, who flourished in the reign of King David I., founded here a Priory of this order, who were dean and chapter of that cathedral. Morice, Prior of this Convent, swore fealty to Edward Langshanks, King of England, in the year 1296. This church was famous for the great resort of pilgrims, who flocked thither from all parts to visit St Ninian's Sepulchre, whom they call commonly the first Bishop of Galloway. We had two famous Priors of this place ; the one called Gavin Dunbar, Prior hereof in the year 1514, and afterwards Archbishop of Glasgow ; the other, James Beton, a son of the family of Balfour in Fife, first, Archbishop of Glasgow, and then of St Andrews, and Chancellor of Scotland."—SPOTISWOOD'S *Religious Houses*, Chap. V. § 3.

severall large and capacious vaults are firme and intire. The Bishop of Galloway, as Prior of Whitherne, hath here a Regality, comprehending, not only the lands about Whitherne, and other adjacent parishes holding of the Prior, but also all the Prior's other lands, which were many in Carrick, Argyle, and severall other places. The Earl of Galloway is Heritable Bayly of this Regality.

It was in this towne of Whitherne, that Patrick Makelwian, minister of Lesbury, in Northumberland, was borne. A wonderfull old man, concerning whom you may have this account, from a letter under his own hand, dated from Lesbury, Octob. 19, 1657, to one William Lialkus, a citizen of Antwerp, which Plempius [as is recorded by Nathan Wanely, in his book, intituled, *The Wonders of the Little World*, Lib. I. cap. 32.] saith he saw under his own hand ; wherein, after he had declared that he had liv'd minister of Lesbury for fifty years, he gives this account of himselfe : " I was," saith he, " born at Whithern, in Galloway, in Scotland, in the year 1546 ; bred up in the Universitie of Edinburgh, where I commenced Master of Arts ; whence, travelling into England, I kept school, and sometimes preach'd, till, in the first of King James, I was inducted into the church of Lesbury, where I now live. As to what concerns the change of my body, it is now the third year since I had two new teeth, one in my upper, and the other in my nether jaw, as is apparent to the touch. My sight, much decayed many years agoe, is now, about the hundred and tenth year of my age, become clearer ; hair adorns my heretofore bald skull. I was never of a fat, but of a slender mean habit of body. My diet has been moderat, nor was I ever accustomed to feasting and tipling. Hunger is the best sauce ; nor did I ever use to feed to satiety. All this is most certain and true, which I have se-

riously, though over hastily, confirmed to you under the
hand of

PATRICK MAKELWIAN,
Minister of Lesbury."

Thomas Atkins, in his letter, dated Sept. 28, 1657,
[recorded by Nathan Wanely (*ibid*) from Fuller's *Wor-
thies*,] declares, that upon a Sunday he heard this old
man pray and preach about an hour and an halfe, making
a good sermon on *Seek ye the kingdome of God, and all
things shall be added unto you ;* and went clearly through
without the help of any notes ; having first read some
part of the Common Prayer, some of holy David's Psalms,
and two chapters, one out of the Old, and the other out
of the New Testament, without the use of spectacles,
the Bible out of which he read the chapters being a very
small printed Bible.   After sermon, the said Thomas
Atkins went with him to his house, who told him, that
his hair (takeing off his cap, and shewing it,) came again
like a child's, but rather flaxen, than ether brown or
grey; that he had three teeth come within these two
years, not yet to their perfection ; while he bred them
he was very ill.   Fourty years since he could not read
the biggest print without spectacles ; and now he bless-
eth God, there is no print so small, no written hand so
small, but he can read it without them.   For his strength
he thinks himselfe as strong now as he hath been these
twenty years.   Not long since, he walked to Alnwick to
dinner, and back again six north countrey miles.   He is
now an hundred and ten years of age, and ever since last
May a hearty body, very cheerfull, and stoops very much.
He had five children after he was eighty years of age ;
four of them lusty lasses, now living with him ; the other
died lately.   His wife yet hardly fifty years of age.

5

As for this old man, he was born in Whithern, as said is, and hath some of his relations living there at present. There is one of his relations for the present serving the Laird of Barnbarroch, in the parish of Kirkinner. The name they are call'd by in Galloway is Micklewayen, which, according to the true Irish orthographie, should be Macgillwian; for surnames that, in Galloway, begin with, or are commonly pronounced, Mal, or Makel, or Mackle, or Mickle, (all which severall ways they are oftimes both written and pronounced,) should, as I am informed by an ingenuous man that exactly understands the Irish language, be writen Mac-gill, as Mac-gill-mein, M'Gill-roy, M'Gill-raith, names frequent in Galloway, and commonly pronounced Malmein, Malroy, or Mickleroy, or Mickleraith, &c.

Principal edifices in this parish of Whitherne, are, 1. Broughton, about two miles distant from the kirk and town, towards the north-east. This house belongs to Richard Murray of Broughton. 2. Castle Wig, more than a mile distant from the kirk, towards the north. It pertaines to William Agnew of Wigg. 3. The Isle, a good stone house, on the sea-side, just beside the sea-port of Whitherne, called the Isle of Whithern, two miles towards the south from the kirk. This house belongs to Patrick Huston of Drummaston. Neer to this place, at the sea-side, there is the ruines of an old chapel, called the Chapel of the Isle, which, as it is reported, was the first that was built for the service of Almighty God in this part of the kingdom, yea, as some say, in the whole kingdom. There is also, in this parish of Whitherne, a Bailirie, called the Bailirie of Busby, holding of the Bishop of Dunblaine, as Deane to his Majestie's Chapel Royal, whereof William Huston of Cotreoch is Herita-

D

ble Bayly. As also another Baylerie, called the Baylerie of Drummaston, whereof Sir Andrew Agnew of Lochnaw is Heritable Bayly. On whom it depends, I do not well know; however, the minister of Portpatrick, as Commendator of Soulseat, (of which more hereafter,) pretends right thereto.

6. GLASSERTON, commonly call'd Glaston. The Bishop of Galloway is patron of it. The Kirk of Glaston, being a large mile to the westward of Whitherne, will be about nine miles distant from the town of Wigton, towards the south-west. This parish of Glaston hath, on the north and north-west, another parish, call'd Kirkmaiden, annext thereto. On the west end of which parish, is a ruinous kirk, called Kirkmaiden, at the sea-side, going down a cliff, and stands pretty pleasantly; it is the burial-place of the Maxwells of Muireith. In this parish of Kirkmaiden, there is a hill, called the Fell of Barullion; and I have been told, but I give not much faith to it, that the sheep that feed there have commonly yellow teeth, as if they were guilded. This parish of Glaston, or Glasserton, the annext parish of Kirkmaiden being included, is bounded, on the south and west, with the sea; on the north, partly with the parish of Mochrum, and partly with the parish of Longcastle, annext to Kirkinner, from which it is divided in part with the loch, call'd on this side the Loch of Remeston; on the east, it is bounded, partly with the parish of Sorbie, and partly with the parish of Whithern. This parish of Glaston, the annext parish of Kirkmaiden being included, is about five miles in length, and about three miles in breadth, the farthest part of the parish being above three miles distant from the parish-kirk.

The principal edifices in this parish, are, 1. Glasserton, or Glaston, the summer residence of the Earl of

Galloway, and about twelve or thirteen miles distant
from the Clary, his winter residence. This house, it is
about a bow-draught to the west from the Kirk of Glaston, at which kirk there is a vault, which is the burial-
place of the Earls of Galloway. 2. Ravinstone, commonly called Remeston. It is a very good house, belonging
to Robert Stewart of Ravinstone, second brother to the
present Earl of Galloway ; it lys almost three miles from
the parish-kirk northwards. 3. Phisgill, a short mile
distant from the parish-kirk southwards, towards the
sea. It pertains to John Stewart of Phisgill, a cadet of
the Earl of Galloway's family. In this gentleman's land,
under a cliff at the sea-side, in a very solitary place, there
is a little cave, call'd St Ninian's Cave, to which, as they
say, St Ninian us'd sometime to retire himselfe, for his
more secret and private devotion. 4. The Mower. This
house, together with the whole parish of Kirkmaiden, in
which parish this house stands, belongs to Sir William
Maxwell of Muirreith. It is about a mile or thereby
distant from Ravinstone westward, and about three miles
distant from the parish-kirk of Glaston ; nether is the way
thither very good.

These three parishes last described, viz. Sorbie, including the two annext parishes of Kirkmadroyn and
Crugleton, Whithern, and Glasserton, including the annext parish of Kirkmaiden, to which may be also added
part of Kirkinner, are commonly call'd the Machirrs or
Machirrs of Whithern, which word Machirrs, as I am
informed, imports white ground ; and indeed those parishes containe by far much more arable and white land
than up in the moors, though the parishes there be much
larger ; yea, if I count aright, the parish of Monnygaffe
for bounds will be larger than the parishes of Kirkin-

ner, Sorbie, Whithern, Glaston, and perhaps Mochrum too.

7. MOCHRUM. The Bishop of Galloway is patron. This parish-kirk lys more than five miles to the north, westward from the Kirk of Glaston ; four miles westward from the Kirk of Kirkinner, and six miles to the south-west from the town of Wigton. This parish of Mochrum is bounded, on the east, with the parish of Kirkinner ; on the south, with the parish of Kirkmaiden, annext to Glaston ; on the west, with the sea ; on the north-west, with the parish of Glenluce ; on the north, partly with the parish of Glenluce, and partly with the parish of Kirkcowand. This parish of Mochrum is about eight miles in length, and but three miles in breadth ; the farthest part will be six miles distant from the parish-kirk.

Principal edifices in this parish, are, 1. Myreton, pronounced Merton, the residence of Sir William Maxwell of Muireith, and lately bought by him from Sir Godfrey M'Culloch, the Cheife of the family of M'Cullochs. Part of this house is built upon a little round hillock, whereof there are severall artificial ones in this countrey, called Motes, and commonly they are trenched about. This house lys towards the south, a large mile distant from the parish-kirk ; it hath an old chapel within less than a bow draught's distance from it. On the north side of this house, and hard by it, is the White Loch of Myrton ; but why call'd white, I know not, except, as Sir William Maxwell informes me, it be so called, because the water (as he saith) hath this property, that it will wash linnen as well without soap, as many others will do with it ; and therefore, in my opinion, it is an excellent place for whitening or bleeching of linnen, Holland and muzlin webbs. This loch is very famous in many writers, who report that it never freezeth in the greatest frosts. Whether it had that vertue of old, I know not; but sure I am it hath it not now; for this same year it was so hard frozen, that the heaviest carriages might have been carried over it. However, I deny not but the water thereof may be medicinal, having receaved severall credible informations, that severall persons, both old and young, have been cured of continued diseases by washing therein; yet still I cannot approve of their washing three times therein, which, they say, they must do; nether the frequenting thereof the first Sunday of the quarter, viz. the first Sunday of February, May, August, and November; although many foolish people affirm, that not only the water of this loch, but also many other springs and wells have more vertue on those days than any other. And here again we may take notice of another mistake in Speed's lesser map, in which Loch Merton is placed betwixt Cree and Blaidnoch, the ground of which mistake perhaps hath proceeded from a gentleman's house in the parish of Penygham, lying betwixt Cree and Blaidnoch, call'd Merton; but there is no loch thereabout of that name. 2. Mochrum; a good house standing in the moors towards Kirkcowand; it stands betwixt two lochs, and is about five miles distant from the Kirk of Mochrum; it is the principal residence of James Dunbar of Mochrum. 3. Ariullan; an house situated neer the sea-side, about a mile and an halfe north-westwardly from the Kirk of Mochrum, in the way from the Kirk of Mochrum to Glenluce. This house, in the year 1679, appertain'd to Alexander Hay of Ariullan. In this parish of Mochrum, under the cliffe at the sea-side, about three miles distance from the Kirk, in the way to Glenluce, is a little ruinous chapel, call'd by the countrey people Chapel Finzian.

These five parishes last described, viz. Kirkinner, Sorbie, Whithern, Glaston, and Mochrum, are all situated southwards of Blaidnoch, and all of them border upon the sea.

8. KIRKCOWAND, pronounced Kirkcuan. The patronage of this parish-kirk is the same with that of Kirkinner, to which it is adjacent, lying about six miles therefrom, towards the north-west. It was, as old people informe me, long since subjected to the care of the minister of Kirkinner, who preached two Sundays at Kirkinner, and the third at Kirkcuan. This parish of Kirkcuan is about ten or eleven miles in length, and about four in breadth ; the farthest part of this parish will be about seven or eight miles distant from the parish-kirk, which is distant six miles, towards the west, from the town of Wigton. This parish of Kirkcuan is bounded, on the north, with the parish of Cammonel, in Carrick ; on the east, with the parish of Penygham, and separated from it with the river of Blaidnoch ; on the south-east, it is bounded with the parish of Kirkinner ; on the south, with the parish of Mochrum ; on the west, it is bounded with the parish of Glenluce, from which it is partly separated by the water of Tarffe, which beginning about the upper end of this parish of Kirkcuan, divides the same from the parish of Glenluce, till at length it turnes more eastwardly, and runnes through part of this parish of Kirkcuan ; and running on the south side of, and neer to, the said kirk, empties itselfe more than halfe a mile beneath the same, into the river of Blaidnoch.

There is but one house of note in this parish, viz. Craichlaw ; a good house, situated about a mile towards the west from the kirk, and is the residence of William Gordon of Craichlaw.

These eight parishes last described, viz. Penygham, Wigton, Kirkinner, with Longcastle annext thereto, Sorbie, with Kirkmadroyn and Crugleton annext to it, Whitherne, Glasserton, with Kirkmaiden annext thereto, Mochrum, and Kirkcowand, in the Shire, together with Monnygaffe in the Stewartry, make up the Presbytry of Wigton, another of the Presbytries pertaining to the Dioces of Galloway. The ministers of the Presbytry meet ordinarly at Wigton once a month, upon a Wednesday, and oftner, as they find occasion for exerceing of church discipline, and other affaires appertaining unto them.

9. GLENLUCE; i. e. *Vallis Lucis*, or *Vallis Lucida*, a pleasant valley, for such it is; or *Vallis Sancti Lucæ*, or *Sanctæ Luciæ;* which of these I shall not positively determin; but however, questionless, it ought to be spell'd Glenluce, and not Glenlus, as Speed and severall others spell the same. It is a large parish, being bounded, on the east, with the parishes of Kirkcuan and Mochrum; on the south, partly with the sea, and partly with the parish of Stoniekirk, from which it is separated by the river of Paltanton; on the west, with the parish of the Inch; on the north, with the parish of Cammonel, in Carrick. The Bishop of Galloway is patron of this parish. The kirk is twelve miles distant from Wigton, westward in the way from thence to Stranrawer, which is six miles farther westward; the farthest part in this parish is about eight or nine miles distant from the parish-kirk.

In this parish, about halfe a mile or more northward from the parish-kirk, is the Abbacy of Glenluce[1] situated in a very pleasant valley, on the east side of the river of Luce ; the steeple, and part of the walls of the Church, together with the Chapter-house, the walls of the Cloyster, the Gate-house, with the walls of the large precincts, are for the most part yet standing. In this parish of Glenluce, there was a spirit, which for a long space molested the house of one Campbell, a weaver ; it would be tedious to give a full relation of all the stories concerning it. Sinclair, in his Hydrostaticks, gives some account of it.

This parish was, in *anno*   , divided into two parishes ; the one call'd the New parish, and the other the Old ; and for that effect, there was a new kirk built about three miles from the other northward ; but at present the saids two parishes are incorporated into one as at first. The whole parish of Glenluce holds of the Bishop of Galloway, as Abbot of Glenluce, who hath a Regality here. Sir John Dalrymple, younger of Stair, is Heritable Bayly thereof. This office is at present exerc'd by Sir Charls Hay of Park.

[1] " Glenluce, or *Vallis Lucis*, in Galloway, gives name to a considerable bay in that country, and was an Abbey, founded in the year 1190, by Rolland, Lord of Galloway, and Constable of Scotland. The monks of this monastery were brought from Melross. Walter, Abbot of this place, was sent to Scotland by John Duke of Albany. Laurence Gordon, son to Alexander, Bishop of Galloway and Archbishop of Athens, was likewise an Abbot of this place. King James VI. erected in his favours Glenluce into a Temporalty, in the year 1602, which was confirmed by act of Parliament 1606. After his death, John Gordon, Dean of Salisbury, son to the said bishop, fell to be Lord Glenluce, and disponed the Lordship to Sir Robert Gordon, his son-in-law. Afterwards Glenluce was united to the Bishoprick of Galloway by act of Parliament ; and at length Sir James Dalrymple, President of the Session, a gentleman of an ancient family in Carrick, was created Lord Glenluce. His son Sir John Dalrymple, King's Advocate, Justice-Clerk, and Secretary of State, was likewise Lord Glenluce and Earl of Stair."—SPOTISWOOD's *Religious Houses*, Chap. IX. § 7.

Principall edifices in this parish, are, 1. Corsecrook, an house standing in the Moor, two miles distant from the kirk eastwards. It was long since pertaining to the Lairds of Barnbarroch ; for the present, it pertaines to Sir James Dalrymple of Stair, who hath lately built it *de novo,* and hath erected here a stately house, according to the moderne architecture, although it might have been more pleasant, if it had been in a more pleasant place. 2. The Park, a very pleasant dwelling, standing on a level hight in the midst of a little wood, upon the west side of the water of Luce, the kirk being opposit thereto on the east side ; it belongs to Sir Charles Hay of Park. 3. Balcarrie ; it is about a mile from the kirk towards the south ; it belongs also to Sir Charles Hay of Park. 4. Schinnernes ; a good stone-house, standing neer the sea upon a promontorie, about two miles from the kirk towards the south-east ; it belongs to the representatives of Kennedy of Schinnernes. Middway betwixt Balcarrie and Schinnernes, and about halfe a mile from each, there is an old chapel or kirk, call'd Kirkchrist, but now it is ruinous.

10. INCH. The Bishop of Galloway is patron of this kirk, which is sixteen miles distant from Wigton, and four miles from Glenluce towards the west, and two miles distant from the town of Stranrawer eastwardly. This parish of the Inch is bounded, on the east, with the parish of Glenluce ; on the south, with the parish of Stoniekirk, from which it is divided by the water of Paltanton ; on the south-west, it is bounded with the parish of Portpatrick, which parish was once belonging to, and was a part of the parish of Inch, and to this day is yet called the black quarter thereof ; on the west, it is bounded with the parish of Laswalt, or Laswede, joyning thereto just at the south side of the town of Stranrawer, which

also bounds the parish of Inch on the west; on the north-west, it is bounded with a great loch or bay of the sea, call'd Loch Rian, pronounced Loch Ryan; on the north, it is bounded with the parishes of Ballantrea and Cammonell, in Carrick; the farthest part of this parish is about six miles distant from the parish-kirk.

In this parish, about a mile from the kirk, towards the south-west, there is the ruines of an Abbacy, environed almost with a great fresh-water loch, in fashion of an horse-shoe. This Abbacy is commonly call'd Salsyde;[1] by Speed Salsid, though by him misplac'd; *potius* Soul Seat, *Sedes Animarum;* some say it should be Saul Seat, *Sedes Saulis,* one Saul being, as they say, Abbot or Monk thereat. The manse belonging to the minister of the Inch is seated here, though a mile distant from the kirk; and the gleib is environed with this loch, and a short trench drawn from one corner to the other thereof. At this manse is a stone pretty large, which I have seen, to the particles whereof broken off, the countrey people attribute great vertue for cureing of the gravel; and tell a long story concerning the progress of that stone, and how it came there, concerning which, if you think fit, you may enquire at Mr James Hutcheson, minister of

---

[1] " Souls-Seat, (called *Sedes animarum,* or *Monasterium viridis stagni,*) in Galloway, near Stranrawer. St Malachias, an Irishman, is said to have founded here the first Community, which is surely a mistake; for it is certain, that the first Religious of this Order were brought here directly from Præmontré, in France, as Johannes le Page relates, in his *Biblioth. Præmonst.* Lib. I. p. 333. It was the Mother of Holywood and Whitehorn, and was founded by Fergus, Lord of Galloway, who became a Canon-Regular in the Abbacy of Holyrood-house, in the year 1160, after he had founded several abbeys and religious places, and endowed them with considerable revenues for the subsistence of the Canons or Monks, whom he brought home and settled in Galloway."—SPOTISWOOD'S *Religious Houses.* Chap. V. § 1.

North Leith, who was a considerable space minister of this parish, and dwelt in this house.

Principal edifices in this parish of the Inch, are, 1. Castle Kennedy, a stately house, and formerly one of the dwelling-houses of the Earls of Cassillis, who long since had great power in Galloway, which occasioned then the ensuing rhyme :—

> " 'Twixt Wigton and the town of Air,
> Portpatrick and the Cruives of Cree,
> No man needs think for to 'bide there,
> Unless he court with Kennedie."

This house now belongs to Sir John Dalrymple, younger of Stair ; it is environed also with a large fresh-water loch, and almost situated like the Abbacy of Soul Seat ; it hath also gardens and orchards environed with the loch. In this loch, there are two severall sorts of trouts ; the one blacker than the other, and each keep their own part of the loch ; so that, when they are in the dish at the table, those that are acquainted with their differences can easily tell in which part of the loch such and such a fish was taken. Just on the other side of the loch, towards the north-west, stands the parish-kirk of the Inch, so call'd from a 'little island, call'd the Inch, situated in the loch, a little distance from the kirk. Within this little island, which is also planted with trees, is a little house built, into which the late Earl of Cassillis us'd to retire himselfe betwixt sermons, having a boat for that purpose, in which also he could be soon transported from Castle Kennedy to the church, and so back again ; the way from the kirk to the Castle by land being about a mile on either side of the loch. 2. Indermessan, situated neer Loch Ryan, about two miles distant from the kirk, towards the north-west. This house belongs to

Sir Andrew Agnew of Lochnaw. Here is a little hamlet or village, which of old was the most considerable place in the Rinds of Galloway, and the greatest town thereabout, till Stranrawer was built. 3. Larg, distant about two miles from the kirk north-east, the residence of William Lin of Larg. 4. Craigcaffie, distant two miles from the kirk north-west, it being not far from Indermessan; it is the residence of Gilbert Neilson of Craigcaffie.

11. STRANRAWER, called also the Chapel. This is a Burgh Royal lately enroll'd. They choose annually a Provest, two Baylys, a Dean of Guild, and a Treasurer, with severall other Councellours. This town is eighteen miles westward from Wigton; it lys upon the bay called Loch Ryan, and is commodiously seated for trade by sea; it is but a little town, yet it is indifferently well built; their houses are within for the most part kept neat and clean, and their meat well dress'd, by reason of their correspondence with Ireland, being only about four miles distant from Portpatrick. They have a considerable market here every Fryday, and two yearly faires; the one being on the first Fryday of May, and the second being on the last Fryday of August, and call'd St John's Fair in harvest. The parish is of a small extent, having nothing but the town belonging thereto; being environ'd with the parish of Laswalt, on the west and south-west; and with the parish of the Inch, on the east and south-east, which two parishes meet at the south side of the towne, and out of these two parishes this parish of Stranrawer is erected; on the north side, it lys open to the Loch Ryan. The Bishop of Galloway is patron hereof.

On the east end of the town, there is a good house pertaining to Sir John Dalrymple, younger of Stair, call'd the Castle of the Chapel, where also there is a chapel now ruinous, from whence all on the east side of the bourn is called the Chapel. Betwixt this house and the kirk, there runns a bourn or strand, so that perhaps the town should be spell'd Strandrawer. This house and the crofts about it, though I have diligently enquir'd there-anent, yet I could never certainly learn to which parish it realy pertaines ; some asserting that it belongs to the parish of the Inch ; others, that it belongs to the parish of Stranrawer, though not lyable to the jurisdiction of the burgh there, as some alledge.

In this towne the last year, while they were digging a water-gate for a mill, they lighted upon a ship, a considerable distance from the shore, unto which the sea, at the highest spring-tide, never comes. It was tranversly under a little bourne, and wholly covered with earth a considerable depth ; for there was a good yard, with kale growing in it, upon the one end of it. By that part of it which was gotten out, my informers, who saw it, conjecture that the vessel had been pretty large ; they also tell me, that the boards were not joyn'd together, after the usual fashion of our present ships or barks, as also that it had nailes of copper.

12. KIRKCOLME, pronounced Kirkcumm. This kirk lys to the north-west of Stranrawer, being about four miles distant from that town, and twentie-two miles distant from Wigton. The Earl of Galloway is patron of this parish of Kirkcolme. It is bounded, towards the south, with the parish of Laswalt ; on all other parts, it is surrounded with the sea ; the farthest part of this parish is about three miles distant from the parish-kirk, which is situated on the east side of the parish, neer the shore of Loch Ryan.

As for edifices in this parish, there is none considerable at present ; but of old there was an house, call'd the

house of Corsewell ; it was a considerable house, but is
now wholly ruinous ; it is neer three miles from the kirk
to the north-west, and lys neer the shore, belonging in
property to the Earl of Galloway, but possess'd by way
of wadset by Mr Hugh Dalrymple.   In this parish of
Kirkcolme, about halfe a mile from the kirk at the Loch
Ryan, there is a place call'd the Skar, which runns into
the sea, and is cover'd at high water ; but at low water,
especially after spring-tides, it will be dry for neer the
space of a mile, upon which oysters are gotten in great
plenty. On the west side of this Skar, muscles and
cockles are also gotten in great plenty.

In this parish also, about a mile and an half from the
kirk, in the way betwixt it and Stranrawer, there was of
old a chapel, called Killemorie, but now wholy ruinous,
within a little croft, of about fourty shillings sterling of
yearly rent, possess'd by a countreyman, John M'Meckin
call'd ordinarly by the countrey people, the Laird, he
and his predecessours having enjoy'd the same for severall
generations.   At the side of this Chapel, in the croft,
commonly called the Laird's Croft, there is a well, to
which people superstitiously resort, to fetch water for
sick persones to drink ; and they report, that if the person's disease be deadly, the well will be so dry, that it
will be difficult to get water ; but if the person be reco-
verable, then there will be water enough.

13. LASWALT, pronounced Laswede.   This kirk lyes
to the north, westward of Stranrawer, from whence it is
distant about two miles, and distant from Wigton twenty
miles.   The Bishop of Galloway is patron.   This parish
of Laswalt is bounded, towards the north, with the parish of Kirkcolme ; on the west, with the sea that looks
to Ireland ; on the south, it is bounded with the parish
of Portpatrick, from which it is partly separated by the

water of Paltanton ; on the south-east and east, it is bounded with the parish of the Inch ; and on the northeast, it is bounded with the Loch Ryan and Stranrawer ; the farthest part in this parish of Laswalt is about three miles distant from the parish-kirk.

Principal edifices in this parish, are, 1. Lochnaw, a very good house, distant from the kirk about a mile westward. This house hath a loch neer to it ; it is the principal residence of Sir Andrew Agnew of Lochnaw. The office of Constabularie is annexed thereto ; and the said Sir Andrew Agnew is Heritable Constable thereof. 2. Galdenoch, a tower-house, more than a mile distant from the kirk north-westwardly, being about a quarter of a mile distant from Lochnaw, towards the north. 3. The Mark, a new house, lately built of brick made there ; it stands about a bow-draught from the town of Stranrawer, and about two miles distant from the parish-kirk. It belongs to Agnew of Sheuchan.

14. PORTPATRICK. The Laird of Dunskay is patron hereof. The parish of Portpatrick is bounded, on the north, with the parish of Laswalt, from which it is in part separated by the water of Paltanton ; on the northeast, it is bounded with the parish of the Inch ; it is bounded, on the east and south, with the parish of Stoniekirk ; on the west, it lyeth upon the sea, and is the usual passage betwixt this countrey and the kingdome of Ireland, from which it is about   leagues distant. The minister of Portpatrick, by a gift from King Charles the Martyr, is Commendator of Soul Seat, and, by vertue thereof, pretends to have a right to several superiorities, priviledges, and emoluments ; but I cannot positively affirme anything thereanent, by reason that his right thereto hath been long in debate before the Lords of Session, and is not yet determined. The Kirk of Port-

patrick stands just on the sea-side, neer to the harbour, which is four miles distant from Stranrawer, and twenty-two miles distant from the town of Wigton, towards the west; the farthest part in the parish of Portpatrick is about three miles distant from the parish-kirk.

Principal edifices, are, 1. Dunskay, once a great castle belonging to my Lord of Airds, in Ireland, now belonging to John Blair of Dunskay, son and heir to Master John Blair, late minister of Portpatrick. It is now wholy ruinous; it stood upon a rock on the sea-side, within a quarter of a miles distance from the kirk. 2. Killanringan, about a mile distant from the kirk towards the north, lying neer the sea-shore, the present residence of the forsaid John Blair of Dunskay, who is heritor thereof, as also of the far greatest part of the whole parish.

15. Stoniekirk. The Laird of Garthland is patron hereof. There are other two parishes annexed to it, viz. Toskerton and Clashshant, both holding of the Bishop of Galloway; upon which account the Bishop alledges, that Garthland should only present at every third vacancy, or at least that they should present *per vices*. This Kirk of Stoniekirk lys to the southward of Stranrawer, from which it is distant about four miles. The parish of Stoniekirk, the other two parishes of Toskerton and Clashshant being included, is bounded, on the east and south-east, with the sands or bay of Glenluce; on the south, with the parish of Kirkmaiden; on the west, with the sea looking towards Ireland; towards the north-west, and more northerly, it is bounded with the parish of Portpatrick; on the north, with the parishes of Inch and Glenluce, from which it is separated by the water of Paltanton; the farthest part of this parish of Stoniekirk, Toskerton and Clashshant being in-

cluded, is distant almost four miles from the parish-
kirk, which is distant, towards the west, from Wigton
eighteen miles.

Principal edifices in this parish of Stoniekirk, are, 1.
Garthland, a good old strong house, distant from the
parish-kirk about a mile north-north-west or thereby.
It is the dwelling-place of William M'Dowall of Garthland. 2. Balgreggan, another good strong house, distant from the parish-kirk a large mile towards the south.
It was the ordinary residence of the Laird of Freuch,
whose sirname is also M'Dowal. 3. Ardwell, distant
from the parish-kirk three miles towards the south. It
is the present residence of Sir Godfrey M'Culloch of
Myrton, and lyes midway betwixt the bay of Glenluce
and the sea looking towards Ireland; the distance betwixt the two seas at high water being about two miles
and an halfe. 4. Killaser, distant from the parish-kirk
about three miles, and about halfe a mile to the eastward
of Ardwell. This house also belongs to Sir Godfrey
M'Culloch.

16. KIRKMAIDEN; so called, because the kirk is dedicated to the Virgin Mary, the print of whose knee is
fabulously reported to be seen on a stone, where she
prayed somewhere about a place in this parish, called
Mary Port, neer to which place there was a chapel long
since, but now wholy ruined. Neer which place also,
at a peece of ground, called Creechen, about a mile distant from the kirk, the sheep have all their teeth very
yellow, yea, and their very skin and wool are yellower
than any other sheep in the countrey, and will easily be
known, though they were mingled with any other flocks
of sheep in the whole countrey. The King's Majesty is
patron of the parish of Kirkmaiden, although the Lairds

E

of Kilhilt pretend thereto, and are in possession thereof.
This parish-kirk is about twenty ⸳⸳⸳⸳⸳ miles distant
from Wigton, towards the south-west, and about
miles distant from Stranrawer, more southwardly. This
parish is an *isthmus,* or narrow tongue of land, reaching
into the sea for the space of about ⸳⸳⸳⸳⸳ miles, and is
surrounded with the sea on all quarters, except at the
one end thereof, which is bounded with the parish of
Stoniekirk. The broadest part of this parish of Kirkmaiden is little more than a mile and an halfe or thereby;
the narrowest part will be about a mile; and the farthest part of the parish will be but a little more than
three miles distant from the parish-kirk. On the point
of this *isthmus,* two large miles and more from the kirk,
and at the south-east part of the parish, is the promontory, call'd the Mule, or Mule of Galloway, to distinguish it from the Mule of Kintyre; at the which place
there is most commonly a very impetuous current.

Principal edifices in this parish, are, 1. Logan, the
dwelling-place of Patrick M'Dowall of Logan, Liveten-
nant to his Majestie's Militia troop of horse for this
Shire, and distant from the parish-kirk about two miles
and an halfe, towards the north. In this gentleman's
land, at the sea-side, opposit to the coast of Ireland, is
a place called Portnessock, very commodious for an harbour; whereupon his eldest son Robert, heir-apparent
of Logan, hath lately procur'd an act of his Majestie's
Privy-Councill, for a voluntary contribution towards the
building of an harbour there. At this Portnessock, there
is an excellent quarrie of slate-stones, which are very
large and durable. The countrey hereabouts, especialy
in the summer-time, is very defective of mills, by reason
that the little bourns are then dryed up; to supply
which defect, the Laird of Logan hath lately built an

excellent wind-mill, which is very usefull, not only to his own lands, but to the whole countrey thereabouts. In this gentleman's land, about a mile and an halfe from the parish-kirk, is a well, call'd Munthick Well; it is in the midst of a litle bogg, to which well severall persons have recourse to fetch water for such as are sick, asserting, (whether it be truth or falsehood, I shall not determine,) that, if the sick person shall recover, the water will so buller and mount up, when the messinger dips in his vessel, that he will hardly get out dry shod, by reason of the overflowing of the well; but if the sick person be not to recover, then there will not be any such overflowing in the least. It is also reported, (but I am not bound to beleeve all reports,) that, in this gentleman's land, there is a rock, at the sea-side, opposit to the coast of Ireland, which is continualy dropping both winter and summer, which drop hath this quality, as my informer saith, that if any person be troubled with the Chine-cough, he may be infallibly cured by holding up his mouth, and letting this drop fall therein. What truth there is in this information, I know not; but this I am sure of, that, on the other shore of this *isthmus*, in this gentleman's ground, there is, or at least not long since was, a salt-pan, where good salt was made with peits, instead of coals. 2. Cloneyard; it was of old a very great house pertaining to Gordon of Cloneyard, but now it is something ruinous; it lyes about a mile distant from the parish-kirk northwardly. 3. Drummore. This house is about three quarters of a mile distant from the parish-kirk, towards the east, and appertaines to Squire Adair of Kilhilt.

These eight parishes last mentioned, viz. Glenluce, the New Kirk being included, Inch, Stranrawer, Kirkcolme, Laswalt, Portpatrick, Stoniekirk, Toskerton and

Clashshant being included, and Kirkmaiden, make up
the Presbytrie of Stranrawer, one of the three Presbytries
of the Dioces of Galloway.   The ministers of the Presbytrie meet ordinarly at Stranrawer, the first Wednesday
of every month, and oftner if they find cause, for exerceing of church discipline, and other affaires belonging to
them.

The sixteen parishes last described, viz. 1. Penygham ; 2. Wigton ; 3. Kirkinner, Longcastle being included ; 4. Sorbie, Kirkmadroyne and Crugleton being
included ; 5. Whitherne ; 6. Glasserton, Kirkmaiden
being included ; 7. Mochrum ; 8. Kirkcowan ; 9. Glenluce, including both the Old and New Kirk ; 10. Inch ;
11. Stranrawer ; 12. Kirkcolme ; 13. Laswalt ; 14. Portpatrick ; 15. Stoniekirk, Toskerton and Clashshant being
included ; and 16. Kirkmaiden, are all lying within the
bounds of the Shire of Wigton, and so lyable to the jurisdiction of the Sheriff of Wigton, which office belongs
heritably to Sir Andrew Agnew of Lochnaw, whose predecessors have enjoy'd the same for more than two hundred and fifty years ; but at present that office is exerc'd
by Colonell John Graham of Claverhouse, and Mr David Graham, his brother.   They keep their head-court
at Wigton, and their ordinary courts there too, either
by themselves or their deputs, every Tuesday, except
in time of vacation.   They have another deput also at
Stranrawer, who keeps court there on Frydays, for the
benefit of such as dwell at a great distance from Wigton,
the head Burgh.   The Shire of Wigton sends two Commissioners to the Parliam. or Convention of Estates,
though far less, both in bounds and valuation, than the
Stewartrie of Kirkcudburgh, which sends but one.

The Commissary of Wigton, who hath his dependance
upon the Bishop of Galloway, hath jurisdiction over the

whole Shire of Wigton, and parish of Monnygaffe, in the Stewartrie; so that the Commissariot of Wigton comprehends exactly the whole Presbytries of Wigton and Stranrawer. He, either by himselfe or his deputs, keeps court at Wigton every Wednesday, except in vacation time, for confirming of testaments, and deciding in causes brought before him.

FINIS PARTIS PRIMÆ.

PART SECOND.

ANSWERS TO QUERIES

CONCERNING

GALLOWAY.

THUS much for the particular parishes of the Stewartrie of Kirkcudburgh and Shire of Wigton, which may serve for a general answer to severall of your queries ; and yet I shall, in this Second Part, give a more particular answer to some of them, which could not be conveniently inserted in the forsaid description of the severall parishes.

As to the first Querie, What the nature of the country or place is ?—*Answ*. The north parts, through the whole Stewartrie, are hilly and mountanous. The whole parish of Monnygaffe consists, for the most part, of hills, mountains, wild forrests, and moors. The southerne part of the Stewartrie is more level and arable. As for the Shire of Wigton, the heads or northern parts of the parishes of Penygham, Kirkcowand, Glenluce, &c. are moors and boggs. The southern part of the Presbytry of Wigton, from the Kirk of Penygham to the sea, contains much arable land, especialy in the Machirrs, which, as I said formerly, imports white land. It consists generally of a thin gravelly ground; but, towards the sea-coast, it is deeper, and more inclining to a clay. The Park of Baldone, for the most part, is a plain even ground, consisting of a very rich clay, bearing excellent grass fit for the syth. In this Park of Baldone, the snow uses to melt shortly after it falls; yea, throughout the whole Shire, except in the northern moors thereof, snow lyes not long, but melts within a day or two, unless it be accompanied with violent frosts. The southern part of the Rinns (the Presbytry of Stranrawer lying westward of the water of Glenluce, being commonly called the Rinns or Rinds of Galloway,) is also arable and level, and the land is more sandie than in the Presbytry of Wigton.

Under this head, I think it will not be amiss to inform you, that, although we have mice good store, yet we have no rats, (in this Presbytrie I meane; but whither they are in the Rinns, I know not.) Whither this proceeds from the nature of the countrey, I cannot determine; or whither they will live here or not. However, there is a gentleman in this parish of Kirkinner, who assures me, that, above thirty years since, he saw an innumerable multitude of rats in his barne, which overspread most of his corne there; but they only stayed a day or two, and then evanished; he not knowing whence they came, or whither they went.

In the Shire of Wigton, we have nether coal, nor lime-stone, nor free-stone, nor any wood considerable, except planting about gentlemen's houses; and yet there are very few parishes but have one or two good stone-houses, very well built, wherein a gentleman of a good quality and estate may conveniently dwell. When they build, they furnish themselves with free-stone from England; as for lime, they are supplyed from the Shellbank of Kirkinner, and with timber for building from the wood of Cree, in Monnygaffe parish, which yeelds abundance of good strong oak. Those that live near the coast side, may, if they please, furnish themselves with coales from England; but, for the most part, the countrey, except towards the sea, is well furnished with mosses, from whence, in the summer time, they provide themselves with peits, which are so plentifull, that, in the parishes of Glenluce and Kirkmaiden, they sometimes have salt-panns, and with peits, instead of coals, make salt. In the parish of Whithern, because severall of them are a considerable distance from the peit-moss, they have a fewell, which they call baked peits, which they take out of a stiff black marish ground in the summer time; work them with their hands, and making them like very thick round cakes, they expose them to the sun, and after they be throughly dry, they yeeld a hot and durable fire.

As to the second part of the Querie; What are the chiefe products ?—*Answ*. Neat, small horses, sheep, and, in some parts of the moors, goats, wool, white woollen cloath, beir, oats, hay. Their bestial are vented in England; their sheep, for the most part, at Edinburgh; their horses and woollen cloath at the faires of Wigton; their wool at Air, Glasgow, Sterling, Edinburg, &c. Their wool is of three sorts: laid-wool, moor-wool, and deal-wool. The most part of their laid-wool, call'd in other parts smear'd wool, is in the parish of Monnygaffe, so called, because, about Martimas, they melt butter and tar together, and therewith they *lay*, for that is their expression, or smear their sheep by parting the wool, and with their finger straking in the mixt but-

ter and tar on the sheeps'-skin, which as it makes the
wool grow longer, and so the better for the finester, so
it fortifies the sheep against the frost and snow, which
uses to be far more excessive there than in the lower
grounds. This wool, though far longer than the other
two sorts, will not give so much per stone, by reason
that when the wool is scour'd, and the butter and tar
wash'd out, it will not hold out weight by far so well as
the next sort, viz. moor-wool. This is the best of the
three sorts, being very cleane, because not tarr'd, and
consequently much whiter. The best moor-wool is said
to be in Penygham, Kirkcowand, Mochrum, Glenluce, in
the Shire, and upon the water of Fleet, in the Stewartrie.
The third sort, viz. dale, or deal-wool, is not usualy
so good as the moor-wool, being much fowler than it, in
regard of the toft-dykes which enclose the sheep-folds in
the ground neer the shore, whereas, in the moors, their
folds are surrounded with dykes of single stones, laid one
upon the other.

The oates, in the Shire, are commonly very bad, being
compar'd with the oates of many other shires; having
long beards or awnds; and although their measure be
heaped, and the weakest and worst of their oates, which
they reserve for their horses and seed, be winnow'd and
drawn out, yet three bolls of corne will not yeeld much
more than one boll of good and sufficient meal straked
measure. However, the countrey people have the dex-
terity of making excellent and very hearty meal, I mean,
when they make it designedly, and for their own use,
shelling it in the mill twice, and sometimes thrice, before
they grind it into meal; and then they grind it not so
small and fine, as they do commonly in other parts. It
is fit to be remembred here, that, before they carry the
corne to the mill, after it is dry'd in the killn, they lay it

upon the killn-flour in a circular bed, about a foot thick ;
then, being barefoot, they go among it, rubbing it with
their feet, (this they call *lomeing* of the corne,) and by
this meanes the long beards or awnds are separated from
the corne, and the corne made, as they terme it, more
smod and easie to pass through the mill, when they are
shelling of the corne there.   The ordinary encrease of
this corne is but three for one, which, for they sow much,
will, except in years of great scarcitie, abundantly satisfy
themselves, and furnish the moorlands plentifully with
victual ; yea, and oftentimes they vend and transport
much thereof to other countreys.

In some places, viz. neer the sea, they sow a whiter
and greater corne, which hath a greater encrease both to
the mill and from it.   They begin to plough their oatland in October, and begin to sow in February, if the
weather will permit ; for that maxime of agriculture,
Properata satio sæpe solet decipere, sera semper, suits
exactly with this countrey.   They divide their arable
land into eight parts at least, which they call *cropts*, four
whereof they till yearly.   Their first cropt they call their
lay, and this is that on which the bestial and sheep were
folded the summer and harvest before, and teathed by
their lying there.   The second cropt they call their
awell, and this is that which was the *lay* cropt the year
before.   The third, which was their *awell* the former
year, they call only the third cropt.   The fourth, is that
which was their third cropt the foregoing year ; however
good husbands till but little of this ; and then these cropts
or parts remaine four years at least untill'd after this, so
that the one halfe of their arable land is only till'd yearly,
the other halfe bearing only grass, and, as they terme it,
lying *lee*.

Thus much for their tilling of their oatland ; save

only that, in the Shire, they till not ordinarly with horses, but with oxen; some onely with eight oxen, but usualy they have ten, which ten oxen are not so expensive by far in keeping as four horses, which must be fed dayly with corne; besides the oxen yeeld much more dung. As also, when they grow old and unserviceable, they get a good price for them from the grasiers and drovers.

In severall parts of the Stewartrie, they till with four horses, all abreast, and bound together to a small tree before, which a boy, or sometimes a woman leads, going backwards. In the meantime, another stronger man hath a strong stick, about four foot long, with an iron-hook at the lowest end thereof, with which, being put into another iron, fastned to the end of the plough-beame, and leaning upon the upper end of the stick, and guiding it with his hands, he holds the plough-beam up or down, accordingly as he finds the ground deep or shallow; the land, where they use this sort of tilling, being far more rocky and stonier than in the Shire.

Their beir is commonly very oatie, and in some places mixt with darnel, (which they call Roseager,) especialy in wet land, and in a wet year. This Roseager being narcotick, occasions strangers to find fault with our ale, although it do not much trouble the inhabitants there; but is sometimes thought by them to be no ill ingredient, providing there be not too great a quantity thereof, because, as some alledge, it makes the drink to be the stronger. As for this Roseager, although I do not much plead for it, yet it is not to be imputed to this countrey as peculiar to our beir; for sure I am, as I was some years since riding in Lothian, within three miles of the Ports of Edinburgh, I saw more plenty of it growing among barly there, than I ever saw growing in so little bounds in any parts of Galloway.

However, as for the beir itselfe, it is indifferent good, though not so birthy as in many other places; for its encrease is usualy but about four or five for one, and yet they are abundantly able to serve themselves, and to transport great quantities thereof to the moors of Monnygaffe, &c. as also to Greenock, and other places. They sow, contrary to their sowing of oates, the best seed they can get, and yet it comes up oatie, much whereof remaines after the winnowing. They deliver to the maltman nine measures of bier, and he delivers back only eight measures of made malt.

They begin to till their beir-land about the latter end of March, or the beginning of April, and after the same hath been till'd about twenty days, and the weeds begin to *plant*, as their phrase is, they sow it, tilling the same but once, which is something peculiar to this countrey; yea, and they sow their beir in the same place every year, and without intermission, which is also peculiar, in a peece of ground lying neerest to their house, and this peece of ground they call their Beir-fay, on which they lay their dung before tilling; but their dung will not suffice to cover the same yearly; yea, they think it sufficient, if, in three years' space, the whole be dunged, and this, I suppose, is also peculiar to this countrey.

After the bier is sprung up, about eight or ten days after the sowing, I have observ'd them towards the evening, (if there hath been a little shower, or they perceave that there will be one ere the next morning,) to harrow their beir-land lightly all over, which, as they find by experience, plucks up and destroys the young weeds, which wither and decay; but the bier presently takes rooting againe without any prejudice, unless a great drouth do immediatly follow. It is frequently observed, that better beir grows on that part of the Fay that was dunged the preceeding year, than on that which was only dung'd the current year. Their bier is ripe about Lambas, and sometimes sooner. They have allways at the end of their Bier-fay, an hemp rigg, on which they sow hemp yearly, which supplys them with sacks, cords, and other domestick uses. This hemp-rigg is very rich land, as being their dung-hill, where they put all their dung, which, in the winter and spring, their byres and stables do furnish them with.

As for wheat, there is but very little of it to be found growing in this countrey. Nether have they any quantity of rye; that which is, is usualy to be found growing with the moor-men only.

As for pease, very few in this countrey sow them; and yet I know by experience, that they might get very much advantage by sowing of them, the encrease being ordinarly sixteen and more for one, yea, and it is a rare thing to see any pease worme-eaten. What the reason is, that they do not sow them, I do not very well know; however, I suppose one reason to be, because their sheep (which are many, and not at all hous'd, as in many other places,) would eat them all up, since the pease should be sowne much sooner than the ordinary time of their herding their sheep.

As to the second Querie concerning plants, I can give no answer save this, that I know no plants peculiar to this countrey; yet I have observ'd these following to grow more plentifully here, than I remember to have seen in other places, viz. At the sea-side, glass-wort, eringo, sea-wormwood, scurvy-grass, sea-kale; and on the rocks, paspier, hind-tongue. In the moors, spleen-wort, heath or hather, with the white flower. In boggs, mosses, and soft grounds, *ros solis*, (the countrey people call it muirill-grass, and give it to their cattel in drink against the disease, call'd the Muir-ill,) *pinguicula*, or butterwort, or Yorkshire sanicle, (which being made into an ointment, is very good to anoint the udders of their kine, when they are hacked or chapped,) *hasta regia*, or Lancashire ashphodele ; as also the true *osmunda regalis*, or *filix florida*, many horse-loads whereof are growing in the Caumfoord, neer the Loch of Longcastle, in this parish of Kirkinner ; this plant the countrey people call the lane-onion, or, as they pronounce it, the lene-onion ; the word *lene*, in their dialect, importing a soft, grassie meadow ground ; they call this plant also by the name of stifling-grasse, and they make much use of it for the consolidating of broken bones or straines, ether in man or beast, by steeping the root thereof in water, till it become like to glue-water or size, wherewith they wash the place affected with very good success. Dane-wort also grows very plentifully on the south-east of Wigton ; in the church-yard of Anwoth ; and in a place of this parish of Kirkinner, call'd the Cruives of Dervagill. This vegitable, whither herb or shrub, I shall not dispute, is found by experience to be very usefull against paines in the joynts, or the contraction of the nerves and sinews, by bathing the place affected, in a decoction of the leaves and stalks of the said plant in sea-water.

I had almost forgot to tell you, that, upon the low rocks covered every spring-tide, in Skelleray, in this parish of Kirkinner, I found the sea-lavender, or *limonium*, which Gerrard calls *Britannica ;* it is a fine plant, with a pretty flower. I took up some of the plants, with the clayie-sand sticking to the roots, and planted the same in my garden, which grew well enough. I have seen this plant since, growing in Mr Sutherland's garden, who told me he brought it from Gravesend.

In the parish of Monnygaffe, there is ane excrescence,

which is gotten off the Craigs there, which the countrey people make up into balls ; but the way of making them I know not ; this they call cork-lit, and make use thereof for litting or dying a kind of purple colour. There is also in the said parish another excrescence, which they get from the roots of trees, and call it woodraw ; it is a kind of fog or moss, with a broad leaf ; this they make use of to lit or dy a kind of orange or philamort colour.

I shall end this head by telling you, that the year after our arable land is turned into grass, it abounds and is almost overspread with *digitalis*, or fox-gloves ; the countrey people call them fox-tree leaves, or deadmen's fingers, some whereof have white flowers ; as allso with a small sorrell, and very commonly also with the lesser *asperula*, and with *ornithopodium*, or birds'-foot, by which you may easily guess at the nature of the ground.

As concerning animals, I can say nothing, save that this countrey, consisting both of moors and valley grounds along the sea-shore, we have such as are usualy found in the like places ; as in the moors, we have plenty of moor-fowles, partridges, tarmakens, &c. In our hills and boggs, foxes, good store. In our lochs and bourns, otters ; neer the sea, severall sorts of wild-geese, wild-ducks, ateales, small teales, sea-maws, gormaws, and an other fowl, which I know not the name of ; it is about the bigness of a pigeon ; it is black, and hath a red bill. I have seen it haunting about the Kirk of Mochrum.

As to the third Querie concerning forrests, I can say but little, save that there is, in the parish of Monnygaffe, a forrest or two, wherein are also some deer ; but of their bounds or jurisdictions, I cannot give any certain or particular account. There is also in the parish of Sorbie, betwixt the Kirks of Kirkinner and Sorbie, a large moor, called the Forrest Moor ; but why so called, I know not,

except it be, as the people say, because there was long
since a great wood growing therein, though at present
there is not one tree growing there, unless two or three
bushes may be call'd so. And here I shall add, that up
and down the whole countrey, I have observ'd many
hawthorne-trees growing in severall places, the boughs
or branches of which trees, (and many times the bole
too,) I have observed growing, or inclining towards the
south-east. The countrey people commonly account the
cutting down of those trees ominous, and tell many stories of accidents that have befallen such as attempted
it, especialy those trees of the greater sort. Why they
have such a regard to those trees, I know not; only
I remember to have read in Heylen, in his Description
of Ægypt, who, speaking of the palm-tree, tells us, that
the nature thereof is, that, though never so ponderous a
weight were put upon it, it yeelds not to the burden, but
still resists the heavines of it, and endeavours to lift and
raise itselfe the more upwards; for which cause, saith
he, it was planted in church-yards, in the easterne countreys, as an emblem of the resurrection; instead whereof
we use the ewe-tree in these cold regions; thus Heylen.
I have indeed observ'd the ewe-tree planted in church-
yards, as also very often the hawthorne-tree, which is also
something of the nature of the palm-tree, upon which
account perhaps at first the people had a respect thereto,
and now esteem it ominous to cut it down.

As to that part of the Querie concerning springs and
their medicinal qualities, I can say nothing, save only
what hath been said in the description of the severall
parishes; as also that there are very many excellent
springs in this countrey, affording great plenty of excellent good water. Severall of them the countrey people,
according to their fancy, alledge to be usefull against

severall deseases, being made use of on such particular
days of the quarter, which superstitious custome I cannot allow of; and yet I doubt not but there are severall
medicinal wells in this countrey, if they were sought out,
and experimented by men capable to judge thereanent.

As to that part of the Querie concerning parks, I can
only say, that the Park of Baldone is the chiefe, yea, I
may say, the first, and as it were the mother of all the
rest, Sir David Dunbar being the first man that brought
parks to be in request in this countrey; but now many
others, finding the great benefit thereof, have followed
his example; as the Earl of Galloway, Sir William
Maxwell, Sir Godfrey M'Culloch, Sir James Dalrymple,
the Laird of Logan, and many others who have their
parks, or enclosed grounds, throughout the whole Shire.

As concerning rivers, the principal are Orr, Kenn,
Dee, Fleet, Cree, Blaidnoch, Luce or Glenluce, and
Paltanton.

ORR hath its rise from Loch Urr or Loch Orr, which
loch is situated betwixt the parish of Balmaclellan, on
the west side, and the parishes of Glencairn and Dunscore, on the east side. In this loch, there is an old ruinous castle, with planting of sauch or willow-trees for the
most part about it, where many wild-geese and other
water-fowles breed; to this place there is an entrie,
from Dunscore side, by a causey, which is covered with
water knee-deep. This loch is replenished with pikes;
many salmon also are found there at spawning-time. From
this loch the river of Orr comes, and dividing the parishes
of Glencairn, Dunscore, Kirkpatrick Durham, Orr, and
Cowend, on the east side, from the parishes of Balmaclellan, Partan, Corsemichael, Bootle, and a point of
Dundranen, on the west side, empties itself into the sea,

F

betwixt Cowend on the one side, and Bootle and a point
of Dundranen on the other side.

This river is observ'd to be in all places of it, both
from head to foot, about twelve miles distant from the
towne of Dumfreis, except you go from the foot of Cowend, under the Fell call'd Cruffald-fell, by the way of
Kirkbeen,
way, and then it will be fourteen distant from it and the
town of Dumfreis. This river is foordable in many
places ; being foordable also
when the tide obstructs not, although, at spring-tides,
the sea-water flows up
However, if the water be at any time great, there is a
stone-bridge over it, call'd the Bridge of Orr, which
joynes the parishes of Kirkpatrick Durham and Corsemichael together.

KENN hath its rise in the Shire of Nithisdale, not far
from the head of the water of Skar, in the said Shire,
and running westward, divides the parish of Corsefairn
from Dalry, and then turning southward, it divides the
parishes of Dalry and Balmaclellan from the parish of
the Kells. It joynes with the river of Dee at a place
called the boat of the Rone, four miles beneath the New
Town of Galloway.

DEE hath its rise from Loch Dee, at the head of the
parish of Monnygaffe, bordering upon

and comeing from thence, hath on the west side the parishes of Monnygaffe, Girthton, Balmaghie, Tongueland,
Twynam, and part of Borgue ; on the east side, it hath
the parishes of Corsefairne, Kells, Partan, Corsemichael,
Kelton, Kirkcudburgh, and empties itselfe into the sea,
about two miles beneath the town of Kirkcudburgh, at
an island, call'd the Ross.

This river is navigable by ships of a great burthen, from its mouth to the towne of Kirkcudburgh and higher. This river is abundantly plenished with excellent salmon. Towards the mouth whereof, Thomas Lidderdail of Isle hath a large fish-yard, wherein he gets abundance of salmon, and many other fish. Two miles above the said town of Kirkcudburgh, at the Abbacy of Tongueland, just where a rivulet, called the water of Tarffe, empties itselfe into the river of Dee, are great rocks and craigs, that, in a dry summer, do hinder the salmon from going higher up; and here it is that the Vicecount of Kenmuir, as Bayly to the Abbacy of Tongueland, hath priveledge of a Bayly-day, and fenceth the river for eight or ten days in the summer-time, prohibiting all persons whatsoever to take any salmon in that space; so that, at the day appointed, if it have been a dry season, there is to be had excellent pastime; the said Vicecount, with his friends, and a multitude of other people, coming thither to the fishing of salmon, which being enclosed in pooles and places among the rocks, men go in and catch in great aboundance, with their hands, speares, listers, &c. yea, and with their very dogs.

At this place, upon the rocks, on the river side, are a great variety of very good herbs growing. I have heard it reported, how true I know not, that it was this place, and the situation thereof, which contributed towards the quickning of Captain Alexander Montgomerie his fancie, when he compos'd the poem, intituled *The Cherie and the Slae.*

In this river, about Balmaghie, are sometimes gotten excellent pearles out of the great muscle; and I am informed, that Master Scot of Bristow hath one of them of a considerable value. In this river is an island, call'd the Threave; but of this I have already spoken in the description of the parish of Balmaghie.   About

above the said island of the Threave, this river is a deep
loch, which loch extends itselfe into the river of Kenn,
and reaches as far as the Castle of Kenmuir, so that the
Vicecount of Kenmuir may easily transport himselfe and
furniture by boat from his Castle of Kenmuir, in the parish of the Kells, to another residence of his in the parish
of Corsemichael, called the Greenlaw, lying on the east
side of Dee ; yea, so neer to it, that sometime the inundation of the river comes into his cellars and lower roomes.
The distance betwixt the saids two houses of Kenmuir
and Greenlaw, which is also the length of the said loch,
will be about eight miles.

FLEET.   This river hath its rise in the parish of
Girthton, and dividing the parish of Girthton, on its
east side, from the parish of Anwoth, on its west side,
empties itselfe into the sea, neer the Castle of Cardonnes,
in the parish of Anwoth. This river, towards the mouth
of it, abounds with many good fish ; also at the mouth
of it, are some little islands, call'd the Isles of Fleet.

CREE.   This river hath its rise from Lochmuan, in
the parish of Cammonell, in Carrick, and dividing the
parishes of Monnygaffe and Kirkmabreck, on its east side,
from the parishes of Cammonell and Penygham, on its
west side, empties itselfe into the sea beneath Wigton. In
that part of this river which divides Cammonell from
Monnygaffe, I have seen severall pearles taken out of the
great muscle.

There is another river, called Munnach, which hath
its rise from the hills of Carrick, and after many flexures
and turnings, (for in the road betwixt the Rowne-tree
Bourne, in Carrick, and Palgowne, in Monnygaffe parish, which will be about the space of four miles, this
river of Munnach is cross'd, if I remember right, about

sixteen or seaventeen times,) it empties itselfe into the
river of Cree, at a foord call'd the Blackwrack, about six
miles from Monnygaffe; at which place beginns the loch
of Cree, about three miles long or thereby; at the foot
whereof, William Stewart of Castle-Stewart hath cruives,
wherein he gets good salmon. Upon the east bank of
this loch, grows that excellent oak wood, which I spoke
of in the description of the parish of Monygaffe; opposit
whereunto, viz. on the west side of the said loch, in the
parish of Penygham, the said William Stewart hath a
wood, which in time may produce good timber; but is
far inferior to the other.

There is another rivulet, called Pinkill Bourn, that,
having its rise in the said parish of Monnygaffe, empties
itselfe into the river of Cree, just betwixt the town and
church of Monnygaffe; and here again are good salmon
caught with nets; as also at other places betwixt the
towne of Monnygaffe and Macchirmore, at which place,
being about a short mile distant from Monnygaffe, there
is a foord, call'd the Foord of Macchirmore, unto which
the tide comes, and to which little barks may come also,
though more than six miles from the sea in *rectâ lineâ*;
but much farther, if we count the flexures of the said
river, which at high water do something resemble the
crooks of the water of Forth betwixt Sterling and Alloa.
This foord is the first foord from the mouth of Cree, except the foord against Wigton, of which more hereafter.
At this foord of Macchirmore, in the month of March,
are usualy taken great quantities of large spirlings; the
head of this fish, when boyl'd, hath been observ'd to
yeeld severall little bones, resembling all the severall sorts
of instruments that shoemakers make use of. Two miles
beneath this foord of Macchirmore, there is another rivulet, call'd Palnure, which empties itselfe into the river

of Cree; it hath its rise in the hills of Monnygaffe; and four miles distant from the towne of Monnygaffe, it runns over a precipice betwixt two rocks, and is call'd there the Gray-mare's Tail, which is just beside a great rock, call'd the Saddle-Loup; at which, it being the road-way, horsemen must alight, for fear of falling off their horses, or rather least horse and man both fall, and never rise again.

And here it is to be observ'd, that, in Timothy Pont's map, (which I have only seen of late, and long after the first writing of these papers,) these two names, viz. the Gray-mare's Tail and the Saddle-Loup are joyn'd together, and call'd by him the Gray Mear's Tail of the Sadillowip; whereas the first, viz. the Gray-mare's Tail, is the name of the water running down betwixt the two rocks, which, in the falling down, resembles the tail of a white or gray horse; and the name of the other, viz. the Saddle-Loup, is the name of a rock hard by, and so called for the reason before specified. Observe also, that the name that he gives it is very ill spell'd; yea, in that map, and in Blaw's map too, which also I have onely seen of late, the names of places are so very ill spell'd, that although I was very well acquainted with the bounds, yet it was a long time before I could understand the particular places designd in that, and in some other of his maps. And hence we may also observe, that, in maps and descriptions of this nature, it is hardly possible, after the greatest care and diligence, to be exact, especialy where we must of necessitie make use of informations, which we receave from severall hands; and therefore these papers, upon the same account, being liable to mistakes, the reader will, I hope, be inclineable to pass them by, they being almost unavoidable.

Beneath the influx of Palnure into the river of Cree,

there is another rivulet, call'd Graddock Bourn, which hath its rise eastward in the great mountain of Cairnesmuir, and dividing the parish of Monnygaffe from the parish of Kirkmabreck, empties itselfe into the river of Cree. This river of Cree, at high water, will be three miles over, as reaching betwixt Wigton in the west, and Kirkmabreck, *alias* Ferriton, in the east; but, at low water, the river containes itselfe in lesser bounds, being not a bow-draught over from the east bank of the Ferriton, to the west bank towards the sands of Wigton.

This place, at low water, is foordable; but I would advise any that comes there, not to ride it, unless he have an expert guide to wade before him, it being very dangerous not only in the foord of the river, but also on the banks thereof, as also in the sands betwixt and Wigton; for, even on the sands about halfe way betwixt the foord and Wigton, there is a bourn, call'd the Bishop Bourn, having its rise in the parish of Penygham, and dividing that parish from the parish of Wigton, empties itselfe into those sands, may occasion prejudice to a stranger, unless he have a good guide.

BLAIDNOCH. This river hath its rise from a loch, called Lochmaberrie, in the parish of Kirkcowan, bordering upon Cammonell, in Carrick, and running southward, divides the parish of Kirkcowan in the west from the parish of Penygham in the east, and then runneth eastwardly, dividing the parish of Kirkinner on the south side from a corner of Penygham, and the parish of Wigton on the north, and running on the south side of the towne of Wigton, empties itselfe into the sea, or else into Cree, on the sands of Wigton.

There is a lesser rivulet, call'd the water of Tarffe, that hath its rise about the north-west part of Kirkcowan, and for a while running southwardly, divides the said

parish of Kirkcowan from the parish of Glenluce ; and
then bending its streames more eastwardly, it runs wholy
in the parish of Kirkcowan, hard by the south side of the
said parish-kirk, where, at a place call'd Lincuan, the
Laird of Craichlaw hath a salmon-fishing, where sometimes he takes good salmon with nets. From this place
the said water of Tarffe runs still eastward, and a large
halfe mile or more from Linçuan, it empties itselfe into
the river of Blaidnoch. About a mile above the meetings of which two waters, at a place call'd the Mill of
Barhoshe, on the river of Blaidnoch, the said Laird of
Craichlaw hath another salmon-fishing. About two miles
beneath the meetings, the Laird of Grainge hath another
salmon-fishing, beneath which, at severall places in the
said river, the Laird of Dereagill, on Kirkinner side, and
the Laird of Torhouse, on Wigton side, have severall
places where they take salmon by nets, both which Lairds
have an equal interest therein ; and some yeares, by
mutuall agreement, they fish day about ; some yeares
again, they fish together, and divide their fish equaly.

There is also another rivulet, call'd the water of Malzow or Malyie, which hath its rise at the loch of Mochrum, and running eastward, it empties itselfe into the
river of Blaidnoch, about a mile beneath the house of
Dereagill, in the parish of Kirkinner. At the head of
this rivulet of Malzow, are many eeles taken about Martimas, which they salt, with their skins on, in barrells, and
then, in the winter time, eat them roasted upon the coals,
and then only pilling off their skins. This rivulet hath
also plenty of trouts.

There is also another rivulet, call'd Milldriggen Bourn,
that hath its rise above the place of Barnbarroch, the
residence of John Vans of Barnbarroch, in the parish of
Kirkinner, and running eastward, enters into the Park

of Baldone, at the bridge of Milldriggen, and dividing
the said Park of Baldone, after many windings and turnings, empties itselfe into the river of Blaidnoch, just opposit to the town of Wigton. This rivulet is also stored
with eeles and trouts. This river of Blaidnoch is stored
with excellent salmon ; the Earl of Galloway possessing
the whole benefit thereof, from the mouth of the said
river to the lands of Torhouse, in the parish of Wigton.
The salmon-fishing in this river is not very good in a
dry year, especialy from Torhouse and upwards, because
the salmon cannot swim up for want of water ; but in
wet years, it commonly affoords good store.

I remember to have seen a fish, which the fishers took
in their nets, in the salt-water of this river beside Wigton ; they call'd it to me a young whale ; it was about
three or four foot long, smooth all over without scales,
and of a blackish colour, if I remember right ; however,
sure I am it had no gills, but ane open place upon the
crowne of the head, instead of gills. It was a female, the
signe thereof being apparent at the first view ; they made
oyl of it. I got about a pint of it from them, which was
very clear and good, and burnt very well in a lamp. I
also once saw a sturgeon, which some one or other of
Wigton had found dead on the sands there ; it had large
boney scales one it, one of which I have.

About the year 1674, there was a pretty large whale,
which came up this river of Blaidnoch, and was kill'd
upon the sands. I did not see it, but saw severall peeces
of it ; for the countrey people ran upon it, and cut as
much as they could bring away, and made oyle of it,
which many persons got good of ; but I am told, if it had
been manag'd right, and not cut so in peeces as it was,
it might have been improv'd to a far greater advantage.

The oyl that I saw and made use of was very good and clear, and burnt very well in my lamp.

GLENLUCE, or LUCE. This river hath its rise in the parish of Cammonell, in Carrick, and running southwardly to the New Kirk of Glenluce, meets there with another water, call'd the Crossewater, which also hath its rise in the parish of Cammonell, in Carrick; from the said New Kirk of Glenluce, it runnes southward by the west side of the precincts of the Abbacie of Glenluce, and then halfe a mile and more beneath that, on the east side of Park Hay, belonging to Sir Charles Hay of Park Hay, and from thence runs still southward, till it empties itselfe into the sea, on the large and vast sands of Glenluce. Towards the foot of this river of Glenluce, Sir Charles Hay hath a fish-yard, wherein he gets salmon, and sometimes great plenty of herring and mackreels.

PALTANTON. This is a small river, having its rise in the parish of Portpatrick, and running south-eastward, dividing the parishes of Portpatrick and Stoniekirk, on the south side, from the parishes of Laswalt, Inch, and Glenluce, on the north side, it empties itselfe into the sea, on the sands of Glenluce.

This river is not very broad, but it is pretty deep, in regard it runs through a sandie clayie ground; and therefore strangers should have a care, when they ride the foords thereof. This river abounds with pikes, and hath some salmon at the mouth thereof.

As to the fourth Querie, What roads, bays, ports for shipping, &c.?—*Answ.* As for the Stewartry; neer the mouth of the water of Orr, in the parish of Dundranen, or Rerick, not far from a place called Airdsheugh, is a very safe harbour for ships, called Balcarie, not far from which is the Isle of Haston, spoken of in the description of the parish of Rerick. At the mouth of Dee, beneath Saint Marie Isle, where the river will be halfe a mile broad, there is a great bay within land, where whole fleets may safely ly at anchor.

As for the Shire of Wigton ; at Wigton, with a spring-tide, and a good pilot, a ship of a considerable burden may be brought up, and easily disburden'd. Betwixt Wigton and Inuerwell, or Enderwell, in the parish of Sorbie, which, I suppose, will be about three miles in *rectâ lineâ*, at low water, is to be seen nothing but a large plaine of sandie clay ; but at Innerwell, ships of great burthen may safely put in ; from whence, doubling the point of Cruglton, till you come to the Isle of Whithern, the coast is for the most part rockie ; but the Isle of Whithern, haveing a narrow entry, yeelds a safe, secure, and advantageous port to ships of a great burthen against all storms. From thence the coast of Whithern, Glasserton, Mochrum, and part of Glenluce is rockie ; but comeing to the Bay of Glenluce, you will find a large bay, and dry sand, when at low water ; then turning southward, along the coast of Stoniekirk and Kirkmaiden, which runs to the Mule of Galloway, the shore is sandie, and, except at high water, you may ride for the space of twelve miles or thereby, betwixt the sea and shore, upon a plain even dry sand, and hardly so much as a peeble-stone to trouble you. This bay or loch of Glenluce or Luce, Speed, in his maps, miscalls L. Lowys. About four or five leagues distant from this place, in the sea, are two great rocks, though the one be greater than the other, called Big Skarr.

The point of the Mule is a great rock, on which, as I have been often informed, such as sail by it in a dark night have observed a great light, which hath occasioned some to say, that there is a rock of diamonds there ;

however, the sea at this point is oftimes very boisterous. Turning about to the west side of the Mule, towards Ireland, the shore is rockie till you come to Portnessock, in the parish of Kirkmaiden, where Robert M'Dowall, younger of Logan, hath been at great paines and expences to build a port for ships and barks cast in that way. The coast from thence to Portpatrick is rockie. Portpatrick itselfe is the ordinary port, where the barks come in with passengers from Ireland, from whence it is distant, as they say, about ten leagues. From Portpatrick to the mouth of Lochryan, the coast is also rocky. The said Lochryan is a very large bay, wherein an whole fleet of the greatest burthen may cast anchor; it will be about two miles or thereby over at the mouth; but then it will be about six or seaven miles long, and about four miles broad. Ships may put to shore at the Claddowhouse, in the parish of the Inch; as also at the town of Stranrawer, which is at the head or south end of the said loch.

As to that part of the Querie, What moon causeth high water?—I cannot give an exact account; but I conceave that a south moon maketh high water about Wigton and Whithern; for I have observed them frequently saying,

" Full moon through light; full sea at midnight."

The seas have plenty of fish, such as salmon, fleuks, solefleuks, turbets, sea-eeles, whitings, &c.; these are taken between Wigton and the Ferriton; some in the halfenet formerly described; some in cups fixt on the sands, neer to the chanel of the river of Cree. On the sands of Kirkinner, are great multitudes of cockles, which, in the year 1674, preserved many poor people from starving. Farther down the sands, neer the sea, they take keilling and skait, by hooks baited and laid upon the sands, which they get at low water. At Polton, in the months of July, August, and September, are sometimes great quantities of herring and mackreels taken with nets. On the coast of Whithern, Glasserton, and Mochrum, they take cronands, codlings, lyths, seathes, or glassons, mackreels by hook and bait in boats, &c. On the mouth of the water of Luce, they take salmon, herring, and mackreels, in a fish-yard belonging to Sir Charles Hay of Park Hay, as I formerly said. On the sands of Luce, they get abundance of the long-shell'd fish, call'd the spout-fish; the man that takes them hath a small iron-rod in his hand, pointed at one end, like an hooked dart, and treading on the sands, and going backward, he exactly knows where the fish is, which is deep in the sands, and stands perpendicular, whereupon he thrusts down his iron-rod quite through the fish betwixt the two shells, and then by the pointed hook he brings up the fish. On these sands, I have seen many shells of severall sizes and shapes; but I pretend no great skill in ichthuologie, and therefore cannot give you their names. In the parish of Kirkcolme, they take many keilling and skait, and sea-carps, with hook and line; they have also there many good oysters, which they get at low water without any trouble. In the loch of Lochrian, there is some years a great herring-fishing; and upon the coast thereabout, they take very good lobsters, and some of them incredibly great. In short, our sea is better stor'd with good fish, than our shoare is furnished with good fishers; for having such plenty of flesh on the shore, they take little paines to seek the sea for fish. I have also heard them say, that it hath been observ'd, that the sea and the land are not usualy plentifull both in one year ; but whither their plenty at land occasions them to say so, I know not.[1]

As to the fifth Querie, concerning monuments, forts, and camps, excepting King Galdus' tomb, already spoken to in the description of the parish of Wigton, I can say nothing, unless it be to tell you, that in a very large plaine, call'd the Green of Macchirmore, halfe a mile to the south, eastward of Monnygaffe, there are severall Cairnes of hand-stones, which, if I mistake not, denote that some great battail or camp hath been there, that space of plain ground being, as I conjecture, sufficient for threescore thousand men to draw up in ; but I could never learn from any person, what particular battel or camp had been there.

I have also observed severall green hillocks, called by the countrey people Moates, as particularly on the west side of Blaidnoch, in the Baronrie of Clugstone, pertaining to the Earl of Galloway ; another at the Kirk of Monnygaffe ; another at the Kirk of Mochrum ; another at the place of Myrton, pertaining to Sir William Maxwell of Muirreith, the one end of the said place of Myrton being built on it ; another neer the house of Balgreggen, in the parish of Stoniekirk, all which have had trenches about them, and have been all artificial ; but when or for what use they were made, I know not.

As to the sixth Querie, concerning battells, I can say nothing. As to that part of the Querie concerning memorable accidents, what I know or have been inform'd of, you may find in the description of particular parishes.

[1] Appendix, No. VI.

As to the seventh Querie, concerning peculiar customes, &c. I have already given an account of their husbandry, and occasionly also of some other things. I now think fit to ad these following particulars :—

Their marriages are commonly celebrated only on Tuesdays or Thursdays. I myselfe have married neer 450 of the inhabitants of this countrey ; all of which, except seaven, were married upon a Tuesday or Thursday. And it is look'd upon as a strange thing to see a marriage upon any other days ; yea, and for the most part also, their marriages are all celebrated *crescente luna.*

As for their burials, I have not observed any peculiarity in them save this, which I have frequently observed at the burialls of the common people, viz. As soon as ever the dead corp is taken out of the house, in order to its carrying to the church-yard, some persons left behind take out the bed-straw, on which the person dyed, and burne the same at a little distance from the house. There may be perhaps some reason for the burning thereof to prevent infection ; but why it should be don just at that time, I know not well, unless it be to give advertisement to any of the people who dwell in the way betwixt and the church-yard, to come and attend the buriall.

The common people are, for the most part, great chewers of tobacco, and are so much addicted to it, that they will ask a peece thereof even from a stranger, as he is riding on the way ; and therefore let not a traveller want an ounce or two of roll-tobacco in his pocket, and for an inch or two thereof, he need not fear the want of a guide either by night or day.

The moor-men have a custome of barrelling whey, which is thus don : When the whey is press'd from the curds, they let it settle, and then pour off the thin clear whey into a barrell or hogshead, which will work and ferment there ; the next time they make the cheese, they do the like, and so dayly pour in the whey into the barrell till it be full. This they close up, and keep it till winter and spring-time, all which time they have but little milk ; yea, it will keep a twelvemonth, but it will be very sour and sharp ; a mutchin whereof being mixt with a pint of spring-water, makes a drink which they make use of in winter, or at any other time, as long as it lasts.

They have also a custome of tanning cow-hides, for their owne and their families' use, with hather instead of bark, which is thus done : Having lim'd the hides, and the hair taken off, and the lime well gotten out, and well washed, they take the bark and cropts of sauch, which they boyl very well, with the decoction whereof they cover the hide in a tub, the decoction being first very well cool'd ; this they call a *washing noose*. The next day or two thereafter, they take the short tops of young green hather, and cut it small with an ax, then put a layer thereof in the bottom of a large tub, upon which they spread the hide, and put another layer of hather upon it, and then fold another ply of the hide, and so hather upon it, and then another ply of the hide, till the hide be all folded up ; allways putting green hather betwixt every fold ; then they put hather above all, and then make a strong decoction of hather, which being very well cool'd, they pour on the hides, till they be all covered, and then put broad stones above all, to keep the hides from swimming. When they find that the hides have drawn out the strength of the decoction, or *noose*, as they call it, which they know by the water, which will begin to be very clear, they take fresh hather, and so repete the operation severall times, till the hides

7

be throughly tann'd, which the countrey shoe-makers, coming to their houses, make into shoes for the use of the family.

And here I shall add, that many of the cords, which they use in harrowing, are made of hemp yarne of their own growing or spinning, which they twine, twentie or thirtie threeds together, according to the greatness of the cords they designe to make, and then they twist three ply of this together very hard, which done, they let them ly in bark *woose,* which they say keeps the cords the longer from rotting.

Some of the countrey people here, in the night time, sleep not except they pull off not only their cloaths, but their very shirts, and then wrap themselves in their blankets; yea, and I have known some of them, who have so addicted themselves to this custome, that when they watch their cattell and sheep in the folds at night, (which they do constantly from the beginning of May, till the corne be taken off the ground, for fear they should breake the fold-dikes in the night time, and do prejudice to themselves or their neighbours,) they ly on the ground with straw or fernes under them, and stripping themselves stark naked, be the night never so cold or stormie, they ly there, wrapping themselves in their blankets, having perhaps sometimes a few sticks placed cheveronwise, and cover'd with turffs to keep their blankets from the raine.

Some of the countrey people, especialy those of the elder sort, do very often omit the letter h after t, as ting for thing; tree for three; tacht for thatch; wit for with; fait for faith; mout for mouth. So also, quite contrary to some north countrey people, (who pronounce v for w, as voe for woe; volves for wolves,) they oftentimes pronounce w for v, as serwant for servant; wery for very; and so they call the months of February, March, and April, the *ware* quarter, w for v, from *ver*. Hence their common proverb, speaking of the stormes in February, *Winter never comes till ware comes;* and this is almost to the same purpose with the English saying, *When the days beginne to lengthen, the cold beginnes to strengthen.*

The people of this countrey do very seldome, or rather not at all, kill or sell their calves, as they do in other places; so that it is a rare thing to see veale, except sometimes, and at some few gentlemen's tables. They give two reasons for this; one is, because, as they say, the cow will not give down her milk without her calfe, (Mandeslo, in his Travels through Persia, India, and other easterne countreys, relates the like of some place there;) and so, should they kill or sell the calfe, they should want the use of the cow; but this, I suppose, might be helped, would they but traine up the cow otherwise at her first calving. The other reason is of more weight, viz. Since a great part of their wealth consists in the product of their cattel, they think it very ill husbandry to sell that for a shilling, which, in three years' time, will yeeld more than twenty.

The weight, by which they sell butter, cheese, tallow, wool, and flax of their owne growth, is by the stone of Wigton, which consists exactly of twentie-two pound and an halfe Trois, and of this they will give you down weight.

The measure, by which they sell their beir, malt, and oates, is their halfe peck, eight whereof make their boll, four their furlet, two their peck. This measure should be burnt and seal'd by the Magistrats of Wigton, and is call'd, in bargains and writen transactions, Met and Measure of Wigton. The quantity of this measure is not exactly knowne, at least it is not allways exactly the same ; for it is hard in this countrey to get two measures exactly alike, the sides thereof being not made of hoops and staves, as the Linlithgow measures are, but of one intire thin peece of ash, bended and nailed together, like the rim of an wool-wheel, and so is apt to cling, and sometimes to alter and change its exact circular frame ; and therefore the countrey people, bargaining among themselves, do usualy condescend upon such a particular measure, that such a neighbour makes use of, to buy and sell with.

The reason of this inequality seems to be a debate betwixt the towne and countrey ; the towne alledging, that the halfe peck should containe sixteen pints ; the countrey, that it should containe only fourteen pints and a chopin ; and then again, suppose they were agreed about the number of pints, yet they disagree about the measure of the pint ; the town alledging, that it should be jugg measure, and some of the countrey alledging, that it should be only pluck measure. However, they sell their beir, malt, and oates by heap, and the vessell is so broad, that the heap will be more than one-third part of the whole. The halfe of this vessell they call an auchlet, qu. an eightlet, or little eight part ; for it is the halfe of that measure, eight whereof make their boll ; so that their boll containes sixteen auchlets ; the furlet eight auchlets ; the peck four auchlets ; and the halfe peck two auchlets. By this auchlet they sell meale, salt, and pease, all straked measure.

About Kirkcudburgh, in the Stewartrie, although their measures are made of the same forme, yet they differ very much as to the quantities, and have another way for counting the divisions of the boll ; but at Monnygaffe, though in the bounds of the Stewartry of Kirkcudburgh,

they count the same way with the towne of Wigton, and
differ very little from their measure, becaus it lyes contiguous to the Shire, and is for the most part furnished
with beir, oates, malt, and meal, from the parishes of the
Presbytry of Wigton, in that Shire, which are all regu-
lated by the met and measure of Wigton.

As to the eight Querie, What monasteries, &c.?—
Answ. Within the Stewartry of Kirkcudburgh, there is,
1. New Abbey,[1] neer Dumfreis ; it, with six churches,

---

[1] " Sweet-Heart, (*Abbacia dulcis cordis*,) in Galloway, called by
Lesly *Suavi-cordium*, was an Abbey, founded in the beginning of the
thirteenth century by Dervorgilla, daughter to Alan, Lord of Galloway, niece to David Earl of Huntingdon, and spouse to John Baliol,
Lord of Castle Bernard, who died in the year 1269, and was here
buried. Andrew Winton, Prior of Lochleven, informs us, that, after
his death, his lady caused take out his heart, and spice and embalm
it ; and putting it in a box of ivory, bound with silver, and enamell-
ed, closed it solemnly in the walls of the church, near to the high
altar, from whence it had the name of Sweet-Heart, which was afterwards changed into that of New Abbey.

" The first Abbot of this place was Henry, who died in his journey
to Citeaux, in the year 1219. He was succeeded by Ericus, *Magister Conversorum ejusdem domus.* Afterwards, John Abbot of this
place swears fealty to Edward Langshanks, in the 1296, according to
Prynne, p. 652, and he is there designed Johan Abbé de Doux-quer.
There is a charter by another John, Abbot of this place, dated at
New Abbey, the 23d October, 1558, and granting *Cuthberto Broun
de Cairn, in emphyteosim, totas et integras quatuor mercatas terra-
rum de Corbully, in baronia sua de Lokendolo, infra senescallatum de
Kirkcudbright ; reddendo annuatim summam octo mercarum usualis
monetæ regni Scotiæ, ad duos anni terminos, viz. Pentecostes, et
Sancti Martini in hyeme.*

" Gilbert Brown, descended of the family of Garsluith, is among
the Monks that assent thereto. He was the last Abbot of this Abbey.
Calderwood, in his History, informs us, that he sat in Parliament the
17th August 1560, whilst the Confession of Faith was approved ;
and in the 1605 he was apprehended by the Lord Cranston, Captain
of the Guards appointed for the Borders, and was sent to Blackness,
and after some days was transported to the Castle of Edinburgh, where
he was kept until his departure out of the kingdom. He died at
Paris, 14th May, 1612. Sir Robert Spotiswood, President of the
Session, and Secretary of State to King Charles I. was designed *Lord
New Abbey,* being then in possession of this dissolved Abbey."—
SPOTISWOOD's *Religious Houses,* Chap. IX. § 12.

depending thereon, viz. Kirkcudburgh, Kelton, Bootle, Corsemichael, Kilpatrick Durham, and Orr, belongs to the Bishop of Edinburgh, and granted to that Bishoprick at its erection by King Charles the Martyr; formerly the revenues thereof were brought in, as I am informed, towards the support of the Castle of Edinburgh. 2. The Abbey of Dundranen, in the parish of Rerick or Monkton; it belongs to the Bishop of Dumblain, as Dean to the Chapel Royal. 3. The Abbey of Tongueland; it belongs to the Bishop of Galloway. The Vicecount of Kenmuir is Heritable Bayly thereof.

In the Shire of Wigton, there is, 1. The Priory of Whitherne; it belongs to the Bishop of Galloway, and hath a Regality annext thereto. The Earl of Galloway is Heritable Bayly thereof. 2. The Abbacy of Glenluce; it belongeth to the Bishop of Galloway. It is a Regality; its jurisdiction reacheth over the whole parish of Glenluce. Sir John Dalrymple, younger of Stair, is Heritable Bayly of this Regality. 3. Salsyde, or Soul-Seat, or Saul-Seat, now allmost wholy ruined; it lyes in the flexure of a loch, within the parish of the Inch. The minister of Portpatrick hath an action in dependance before the Lords of Session, concerning the superiority of the lands belonging to this Abbacy, and is sometimes call'd Commendator of Salside; but what will be the decision thereof, I know not.

As to the ninth Querie, I can only say, that the house of Gairlies, in the parish of Monnygaffe, and the house of Glasserton, in the parish of Glasserton, affoord titles to the Earl of Galloway, whose title is Earl of Galloway, Lord Stewart of Gairlies and Glasserton. The Earl of Galloway his eldest son is call'd the Lord Gairlies. So Castle Kennedy, in the parish of the Inch, affoords a title to the Earl of Cassillis his eldest son, who is stil'd Lord

Kennedy. As also the Castle of the Kenmuir, in the parish of the Kells, affoords a title to the Vicecount of Kenmuir.

As to the tenth, eleventh, and twelth Queries, they are answer'd in the description of the particular parishes.

As for the rest of the Queries, to the nobility, gentry, burrows, as I am not concerned therein, so it would be an attempt far above my capacity to give any satisfactory answer concerning them.[1]

I shall only presume to give some short account concerning the Bishop of Galloway and the Chapter.

As to the Bishop of Galloway, his priveledges and dignities. He is Vicar-Generall to the Archbishop of Glasgow, and in the vacancie of that See, can do any thing that the Archbishop himselfe could have done, viz. Can present *jure proprio* to vacant churches at the Archbishop's gift; can present *jure devoluto* to laick patronages that are elaps'd; can ordain, collate, and institute within the Archbishoprick of Glasgow, &c. He takes place of all

---

[1] William Lithgow, whose *Rare Adventures* were published in 1632, thus notices Galloway :—

" I found heere, in Galloway, in diverse rode-way innes, as good cheare, hospitality, and serviceable attendance, as though I had been ingrafted in Lombardy or Naples."

" The wooll of which countrey is nothing inferiour to that in Biscai of Spaine; providing they had skill to fine, spin, weave, and labour it as they should. Nay, the Calabrian silke had never a better luster, and softer gripe, then I have seene and touched this growing wooll there on sheepes' backs; the mutton whereof excelleth in sweetnesse. So this country aboundeth in bestiall, especially in little horses, which for mettall and riding, may rather be tearmed bastard barbs than Gallowedian nagges."

" Likewise their nobility and gentry are as courteous and every way generously disposed, as eyther discretion would wish and honour command; that (Cunningham being excepted, which may be called the *Accademy* of Religion, for a sanctified clergy and a godly people,) certainly Galloway is become more civill of late than any maritime country bordering upon the westerne sea."—P. 495.

the Bishops in Scotland, except the Bishop of Edinburgh. The coat of armes belonging to him as Bishop of Galloway is *Argent*, St Ninian standing full fac'd *proper*, cloath'd with a pontificall *robe purpure*, on his head a *miter*, and in his dexter hand a *crosier Or*. As for the time of the erection of this Bishoprick, better chronologists and historians, than I can pretend to be, must be consulted.

As to the Chapter, although the King, in his *Conge d'Elire*, keeping the ordinary stile, beginnes thus: *Carolus Secundus Dei gratia, Scotiæ, Angliæ, Franciæ, et Hiberniæ, Rex, Fidei Defensor, &c. Dilectis nostris in Christo, Decano et Capitulo Ecclesiæ Cathedralis Gallovidienses, salutem,* and directs his *literas commendaticias* to our trusty and well-beloved, *the Deane and Chapter of the Cathedrall Church of Galloway;* and although, as I have heard it reported, King Charles the Martyr nominated and appointed the minister of Whithern to be Deane, and mortified a salary for that effect, yet there is no Deane of Galloway; onely an Archdeacon, who is *Archidiaconus vicem Decani supplens.* This is, and hath been in the constant possession of the minister of Penygham; yet he hath no salarie for that effect, nether have any of the rest of the members of the Chapter one sixpence that I know of, or could ever hear tell of, upon the account of their being members of the Chapter. However, upon the King's *Conge d'Elire,* the Chapter of Galloway, upon the Archdeacon's advertisement, use to meet in the Cathedral Church of Whithern, built by Saint Ninian, and dedicat by him, as they say, to his uncle Saint Martin, Bishop of Tours, in France. The bell yet extant (of which I have formerly spoken in the description of Whithern,) makes it evident that the church is Saint Martin's Church. However, the members of the Chapter of Galloway are,

The Minister of	Penygham. *Archidiac.* Whithern. *Pastor Candidæ Casæ.* Wigton. *Pastor Victoniensis.*	These are within the Presbytery of Wigton.
The Minister of	Inch. *Sedis Animarum Pastor.* Stoniekirk. *Pastor Lithoclesiensis.* Leswalt. *Pastor Leswaltensis.*	These are within the Presbytery of Stranrawer.
The Minister of	Kirkcudburgh. *Pastor Kirkcudburgensis.* Rerick. *Pastor Rericensis.* Borgue. *Pastor Borgensis.* Twynam. *Pastor Twynamensis.* Crosmichael. *Pastor Crucemichael.* Dalry. *Pastor Dalriensis.*	These are within the Presbytery of Kirkcudburgh.

As for the number of the parishes in the Diocess of Galloway, they are thirty-four, viz. Within the Presbytery of Kirkcudburgh, seaventeen; within the Presbytery of Wigton, nine; within the Presbytery of Stranrawer, eight. These parishes have been particularly described already, together with severall other little parishes annext to some of them.

As for the Bishops of Galloway, their foundations for publick and pious uses, together with their revenues, I wish I could say more than I can. For such was the sacriledge and irreligious practices of many, both of the clergy and laity, both of the Romanists and Protestants, about the time of the Reformation in Queen Marie's days, that the foundations for pious uses were so diverted from the intent and design of the first founders, that the very remaines and *vestigia* are hardly heard tell of; which no doubt hath occasioned many good Protestant Bishops, that have been there, to dispose of their charity more privatly, and not to lay any found, that I know of, for any pious or publick use, lest it should meet with the like fate. Yea, and for the revenues of the Bishoprick, they were so far dilapidate, that when the civil government thought fit to settle episcopacy, there could not be found any revenue like a competency for a bishop to live upon; and therefore the Abbacy of Glenluce, with the superiority of the lands belonging thereto; the Priory of

Whitherne, with the superiority of the lands belonging thereto; the Abbacy of Tongueland, with the superiority of the lands belonging thereto, were all annext to the Bishoprick of Galloway, to make a competency for him. The King also purchased the patronages and teinds of the kirks of Dumfreis, Trailflat, Closeburn, Staple-Gordon, and Dumgree, all lying within the Diocess of Glasgow, from the Earl of Roxburgh, which five kirks were pendicles of the Abbacy of Kelso, to which Abbey that Earl had a right, and granted the benefit accrescing from these churches (the respective ministers of the saids five kirks being first provided for) to the Bishoprick of Galloway; so that now, although the revenues of the Bishoprick are not large and opulent, yet if times were peaceable, he might live there well enough upon it; and might, moreover, performe such acts of hospitality and charity, as would much ingratiat himselfe with the people of that countrey, had he also but a convenient house to live in. For, as I formerly insinuated, the Bishoprick was so dilapidated, that there is not so much as an house in all the Dioces, that, as Bishop of Galloway, he can call his owne; the pityfull dwelling the Bishops of Galloway of late have hitherto had, being only in a chapel belonging to the Abbacy of Glenluce, and within the precincts of that ruinous Abbey. The Bishop himselfe, when dwelling in the countrey, preaching in the kirk of Glenluce on the Sundays in the forenoon, and giving out of his revenue a salary to a minister to preach for him in the afternoons, the Bishop being present, and to preach both diets, he being absent.

As for the lands that hold of him, as Bishop of Galloway, as Prior of Whitherne, as Abbot of Glenluce, and as Abbot of Tongueland, and as having right to the five parishes above specified, they are very many; but yet considering, that the yeerly dutys payable forth of the lands are very small, as also that these lands are far distant, some of them lying in Annandale, some in Nithisdale, some in Eskdale, some in Argyle, some in Carrick ; together with the set yearly salaries that his Baylies of Glenluce, Whitherne, and Tongueland get from him ; as also the yearly salarie that he gives to his chamberlain or factor, to uplift his revenues, so far scattered from each other, the profit that will come to him *de claro* will not be excessive ; and yet moderat though it be, and may secure him from being pitied, yet it cannot secure him from being envied.

The Bishop of Galloway is undoubted patron of one-and-twentie parishes, whereof thirteen are principall parishes in his own Diocess. 1. Whitherne ; 2. Sorbie, with the two Kirks of Kirkmadroyn and Crugleton thereto annext ; 3. Glaston, with the Kirk of Kirkmaiden annext thereto ; 4. Mochrum ; 5. Monnygaffe. These five are within the Presbytery of Wigton. 6. Glenluce ; 7. Inch ; 8. Stranrawer ; 9. Laswalt. These four are within the Presbytery of Stranrawer, where also we may add other two, viz. Toskerton and Clashshant, which are annext to the parish of Stoniekirk. 10. Tongueland ; 11. Corsefairne ; 12. Borgue, with the two Kirks of Sennick and Kirkanders annext thereto. 13. Girthton. These four are within the Presbytery of Kirkcudburgh.

The other eight are without the bounds of his owne Diocess, viz. 14. Killmoiden, *alias* Glendarwell, within the Shire and Diocess of Argyle, and Presbytery of Cowell or Dinnune. The Bishop of Galloway is patron hereof, as Prior of Whithern ; 15. Kirkmichael. This parish lyes in Carrick, within the Shire of Air, Archbishoprick of Glasgow, and Presbytery of Air. The Bishop of Galloway is patron hereof allso, as Prior of Whithern ; 16. Traqueir. This parish, as hath been said, lys

within the Stewartrie of Kirkcudburgh, and is under the
Archbishop of Glasgow, within the Presbytery of Dumfreis. The Bishop of Galloway is patron of it, as Abbot
of Tongueland. 17. Dumfreis, the head Burgh of the
Shire of Nithisdale, and a Presbytery seat; it lyes within
the Archbishoprick of Glasgow. 18. Trailflat. This parish-kirk is, or at least was, an excellent structure; the
roof thereof being fam'd for the curious and exquisite
architecture thereof; it is now in part ruinous, and is
annext to the parish of Tinnal, both which parishes are
lying within the Shire of Nithisdale, Presbytery of Dumfreis, and Archbishoprick of Glasgow. 19. Closeburn.
This parish lyes within the Shire of Nithisdale, Presbytery of Pinpont,[1] and Diocess of Glasgow; the Kirk of
Dalgarno, whereof the Bishop of Edinburgh is patron,
is annext to this parish of Closeburn. 20. Drumgree.
This parish is within the Presbytery of Lochmaban, in
Annandale, and Diocese of Glasgow. This parish of
Drumgree is annext to the parish of   , except a little part thereof, which, if I mistake not, is annext to the parish of Kilpatrick   , and payeth
yearly, to the Bishop of Galloway, about fourty pound
Scots. 21. Staple-Gordon. This parish is within the
Presbytery of Middlebie, in Eskdale, lying within the
Shire of   , and Diocese of Glasgow. The
patronages and superplus teinds of these five parishes,
viz. Dumfreis, Trailflat, Closeburn, Drumgree, and Staple-Gordon, were pendicles of the Abbacy of Kelso, and
purchas'd from the Earl of Roxburgh by the King, and
granted by his Majestie to the Bishops of Galloway, as
said is, towards the encreasing of their revenue.

The Bishops of Galloway also had of old the patronages and teinds of two parishes in the Isle of Man; yea,
and, as I am informed, were in possession of them since

[1] Appendix, No. VII.

the Reformation; but at present they are worne out of
the possession thereof. The Bishop of Galloway also
pretends that he hath the priveledge of nominating the
Provest of Whithern; for sure I am, when I was there
with him, he refus'd to accept the ordinary complement
from them (which he took from other burghs) of being
made Burgess there, least his taking it from them might
militate against his own right.

And thus, Sir, I have given as full an answer to your
Queries as possibly I can, ether from my own knowledge
and observation, or from what informations I have gathered from others, many of which perhaps may be
founded upon mistakes; but I can assure you, that they
are not *de industria* in me.   However, if this do not satisfy a more curious inquirer, I shall be content to use
my endeavour that he may be better inform'd, and this
perhaps I may hereafter do, by way of an appendix, by
affoording him my help and directions to travel to the
principal places of this countrey, yea, and to Portpatrick
itselfe, (and thence to Ireland, if he please,) from Carlisle,
Edinburgh, and Glasgow.

And now, Sir, if these papers, such as they are, can be
any wise subservient to your designe in composing and
publishing the Scotish Atlas, I shall not think my time
and labour in collecting them hath been spent in vaine;
yea, and I shall be always willing, in my station, to affoord my weak assistance to any publick good, that shall
be carried on by commendable and innocent meanes, as
these of yours are.   Upon which account, I am

Your humble servant in all duty,
ANDREW SYMSON.

KIRKINNER,
ANNO DOMINI, M.DC.LXXX.IV.

APPENDIX,

CONTAINING ORIGINAL PAPERS

FROM THE

SIBBALD AND MACFARLANE

MSS.

APPENDIX.

No. I.

GALLOWAY

TYPOGRAPHISED BY MR TIMOTHY PONT.

Collections on the Scottish Shires,
By Sir James Balfour and Sir Robert Sibbald.
MS. Adv. Lib. M. 6. 15. No. 14.

I.

BRIGANTIA wonne by Galdus, King of Scottis, frome the Romanis, frome quhosse name it wes callid firste Galdia, then Gallauidia, Gallavithia, and vulgarly Galloway.

Eugenius ye V reskewes the castell of Donskene, then the strongest in all Galloway, from Edfred, K. of the Northumbers, quhome he encounteris at the river of Lewis, in Galloway, betwix quhome ther wes foughten a most cruelle batell, quherin Edfred, vith 20,000 Saxonis, ver killed, and 6000 Scottis; A^{no} 2do regni regis Eugenii V.

Mordacus, *Rex Scottorum*, foundet the Abey of Quhet-herne, in Galloway, famous for the mirackellis of St Niniane, *Qui primus Candidæ Casæ fuit Episcopus.*

Nixt adjacent to Carrick layes Galloway, *olim* Brigantia, bordring with Nidisdaile, almost declyning to ye south ; this countrey and shyre being so spatious and large, yat it incloses in effecte all yat syde of Scotland, being [more] plentifull in bestiall then cornes.

Ther is almost no grate hills in Galloway, bot it is full of rockey knowes ; the vatters gathring togidder betwix thesse knoulls, make almost innumerable lochs and standing vasches, from quhence ye first floude yat comes befor the autumnall equinoxiall, maketh such plentey of vatters to flow, yat ther comes out of the standing vatters suche incredible number of eeiles, being catcht by the inhabitantis in creillis ; them they salte and keipis in store for ther vinter provisione, to ther grate commodity.

The [farthest] pairt one that syde is the Head Nouantum of Ptolomey, or ye Mull of Galloway, yat is the Beecke.

In Galloway ar the tounes of Kirkcudbright, being a good merchant toune, fitted with a commodious harbrey and castle ; Vhithorne, or Candida Casa, the seat of the Byschop of Gallway ; Vigtoune, a goodly market toune ; Innermessane, Minnegoffe, St John's Clachan.

Under ye Head Nouantum, ther is a heauen for shippes at the mouth of the riuer Lossie, anciently named *Reregonius Sinus.*

In the other syde of Galloway, ouer against this heauen, from Clydsfirth, ther enters ane vther heauen, comonly named Lochryen, the ancient *Vidogora* of Ptolomey. All yat layeth betwix thesse two heauens or gulffs, the countrey people name the Ryndes, yat is the poynt of Galloway, as Nowantum the Beecke or Nosse.

Religious Places.

New Abey, or Dulcis Cordis, Glenluss, Saule Seatt, or Sedes Animarum, Dundrenan, Tongeland.

Castells and Gentlemen's Housses of cheiffe notte in the countrey of Galloway ar thesse :—

Treue.	Kirkgunze.
Barcloy.	Crowgiltone, seated one a rocke,
Hills.	environ'd withe the sea.
Orchardtoune.	Garlies.
Bomby in Lochfergus.	Large.
Cumpstoun.	Clare, a strange castle.
Cardones.	Dunskay
Wreythis.	Corsell.
Kenmure.	Lochnee.

The gratest Laichs in Galloway ar,

Rubinfranco.

Carlingworke.

Myrteoune, which, in ye most rigide winter, never frises, the vatters quherof ar supposed to be sulpheureous.

Riuers in Galloway of most notte ar,

Vre.

Dee.

Terfe.

Fleit.

Kenne.

Cree.

Losse, wich, all by generall wyndings and turnings, discharge themselues in the Irisch sea.

H

II.

From Nidisdaile, as you goe one vestward ye Nouantes inhabited in the vales, all yat tracke wich runneth out farr and wyde toward the west, betwene Dumbritton firth and ye sea, yet so indented and hollowed with noukes and creekes, yat heir and ther it is draun in a narrow roume, and then againe in the wery vtmost skirt it openeth and spredeth it selue abroad at more liberty, quhervpoune some haue called it ye Chersonesus, yat is the Biland of the Nouantes, which, at this daye, does containe the countries of Galloway, Carricke, Kyle, and Cuninghame.

Galloway, in the Latine writters of the midle tyme, Gaelvallia *siue* Gallouidia, so called, be the Irich, quho sume tyme duelt ther, and terme themselues shorte in ther awen language Gael.

The river Dea mentioned by Ptolomee, keipeth its auncient name heir in Galloway called Dee.

Kirkubright, a brughe, givin the name to ye quholl Steuartrey.

The castell of Cardines seatted vpoune a craigey and heigh rocke, ouer the riuer Fleet, and fensed with stronge walls.

Neirbute it is the riuer Ken, corruptly read in Ptolomee Iena.

Vigtoune a sea toune in this countrey, giving the name to ye Shyre, quhence it is called ye Shriffdoume of Vigtoune. It layes, this toune, betwix the two riuers of Bluidnoo and Crea; the family of ye Agnews ar heritable Sheriffis of Galloway.

Neirbute this Ptolomee placed ye city Leucophibia, therefter ye Episcopall seat of St Ninian; which Beda

calleth Candida Casa, and wee now in this same lettere
Vhitherne.—Quhat say you then if Ptolomee, after his
maner, translated yat name in Greeke ΛΕΥΚΑ ΟΙΚΙΔΙΑ,
yat is whitt housses (in steàd quherof the translauters
haue thrust vpon us Leucophibia,) which ye Picts termed
Candida Casa? In this place, Ninian, a holy man, ye
first yat instructed ye Picts in the Christian faith, in
ye rainge of ye Emperour Theodosius Junior, had this
seat, and bulte a church heir in memorie of St Martine;
and therafter quhen the number of Christianis wer aug-
mented, and ye Christian faith begune to flowrisch, then
wes ther ane Episcopall see erected at this Candida Casa.

A litle heigher ther is a Biland, having the sea insi-
nuating it selue one both sydes with two bayes, yat by a
narrow neck it is ioyned to ye firme land, and this is pro-
perly called Chersonesus sive Promontorium Novantum,
vulgarley, the Mule of Galloway.

Fergus ye first Earle of Galloway Reg: Da: 1 dotit to
ye Monastarey of ye Holycross neir Edinbrughe, Bar-
roniam de Dunrode. He gave for armes a lyone Ram:
Arg: cround *Or,* in a seild *Azure.*

III.

COMITES : GALLOWIDIÆ.

FERGUSIUS I. Com:
Reg: DAVID I.

UTHRED FILIUS NATU
MAX. FERGUSII COM: 2.
GALLOWIDIÆ,
REG. MAL: 4.

ETHREDUS
filius primo genitus
com: Ucthredi

ALANNUS
filius vnicus
Ethredi

GILBERTUS
filius 2dus com: Ucthredi, mortuo
patre, frat: Ethredum prælio
devicit. Orbatus occulis, lingua
privatus, Marte eum tradidit; sed
Gilbertus non diu superstes;
obiit reg. Willielmo rege
Scottorum.

AVITIA
uxor I. nupta
Allano Com:
Gallowidiae,
et Constabul:
Scotiæ

ALLANUS
filius unicus Ethre-
di et heres Vthredi
Com: Gallowidiæ
et Constabul. Sco-
tiae.

MARGARETIA
filia natu maxima
Davidis comitis
Huntingtonii et
Angus frat : Mal:
4, et Will: Reg:
Scotiae, Allani com:
Uxor 2da

HELENA
Allani filia ex prima
uxore, nupta Rogero
de Quincy Com:
Vintoniæ

DERVOLGILDA
Allani com: fil: unica ex
Marga: 2da. uxore; nupta
Joha: Baliolo Dynasta ab
Harecourte et Dampier in
Normannia: ex qua com:
Joh: de Baliolo Coronat:
regem Scott:

ALEXANDER
Senescallus, Baro de Garleis a Ja: 6.
Scottorum Reg: creatus comes Gallovidiae
in A°. 1623.

MONASTERIA IN GALLOWEIA,

ex

Dempsteri Apparat.

Lib. I. Cap. XV.

GLENLUS in *Galweia*, ordini Cistertiensi, erexit vero princeps de Galueia *Rothelandus* filius *Othredi* pater *Alani.*

SEDES ANIMARUM, vulgo *Saulset* in *Galweia* ordini Præmonstratensi fundauit *Fergusius* princeps dicti *Othredi* pater.

DULCIS CORDIS, vernacule *Neuabbey* in *Galweia*, fundator Deruorgilla, filia *Alani de Galweia*, neptis vero Dauidis de Huntinton, qui postea regnauit. Hæc sola penes Abbatem Catholicum, inuitis hæreticis, remansit.

DUNDRAN in *Galweia*. Fundat Cistersiensi ordini S. Dauid, Rex: Hect. Boeth. Lib. XII., Historiæ Scoticæ, pag. CCLXXIV.; ex hoc S. *Richardus Sacrista* fuit, et *Thomas* Abbas Pontificis elector concilie Constantinensi MCCCCXXXIX., qui *Donduno* male ab Onufrio dicitur apud Ioannem Gualterium Chron: Chronicorum, Demochares a *Dundraina* vocat.

TUNGLAND in Gallweia, ordini Præmonstratensi, fundatum a *Fergusio*, principe de *Galweia*, dixi in Script. Scotis.

SACRI NEMORIS, vulgo *Halywood*, fundat in *Galweia*, Dircongal; cujus filius *Ioannes a Sacrobosco* vt probatum multis, Lib. XVI., Scriptor. Scot.

No. II.

DESCRIPTION OF THE STEWARTRIE OF
KIRKCUDBRIGHT.

Description of Scotland ; Sibbald MSS. Adv. Lib.
Jac. 5th, 1. 4.

The Stewartrie of Kirkudbright, which maketh the
lower part of the Shyre, is towards the west divided from
the shyre of Wigtoun by the Water of Cree ; upon the
south, it heth the Irish Sea ; to the north, it marcheth
with Kyle ; and to the east, it marcheth with the shyre
of Drumfriese.

The Water of Dee divydes this Stewartrie in two
parts ; that to the west being included betwixt the
Waters of Cree and Dee, and that to the east betwixt
Dee and the marches of the Shyre upon the east.

The whole taken togither makes the Stewartrie to be
circular ; its centre will be the south end of the great
Loch of Kenne Water, and the most easterly point thereof, which bordereth upon the Airds, a parte of the estate
of Earlstoun. The water of Kenn from its fountain,
whill it meeteth with the water of Dee, and then the
water of Dee to the Isle of Ross, where it entereth into
the ocean, maketh up the diameter of the circle, wherby
the Stewartry is very naturally divided almost in two
equall parts. The diameter itself will be thretty miles at
least.

The head of the water of Kenn lyeth north north east from the Sores and Ross, and the water generally runneth south south west, and the head marcheth with Nidesdale. Then the straightest way from the town of Drumfrise to the village of Minigoff goeth through the foresaid center, and (though it be not the rode way) will almost be equall, very little short of the former diameter, crossing it at right angles ; and Minigoff marcheth with the Shyre of Galloway.

The southern semicircle (whose circumference is from Drumfrise by the Ross of Kirkudbright, round about to Minigoff) is marched with the sea : for the sea floweth at spring tydes to the bridge of Drumfrise, and a little upwards. At spring tydes, also, it floweth to Minigoff village. From Drumfrise to the foot of the river, Nith divideth the Stewartry from Nidesdale ; then Nith entering into Sullway Firth, to the Ross of Kirkudbright it is marched with Sulway Firth. The entry of this firth into the ocean is betwixt the Ross and Saint Beishead, in Cumberland of England, which will be twenty-four miles over.

From the Ross to Minigoff, the Firth of Cree marcheth, whose entry into the ocean is betwixt the Ross and the point of Withern, in the Shyre, called ye Burrow-head, which is twelf myles over unto its head, which is betwixt the town of Wigtoun in the Shyre, and Cassincary in the Stuartry, belonging to ane ancient family of the name of Moor ; and from thence to Minigoff town, being six miles, the water of Cree—both the water and the firth separating the Stewartry from the Shyre of Wigtoun.

The thrid quadrant, which is betwixt Minigoff and the head of Kenn, is yet devyded by the water of Cree from the Shyre, afterward by a dry march to ye great loch of Dun, which separateth it also from Caricke. Then Kyle, near to ye foot of the Lough, marcheth the Stuartry with a dry march near to the head of Kenn, wher Niddesdale cometh to march.

The fourth quadrant, which is to the north-east, is betwixt the head of Kenn and Drumfris; it marcheth all alongst with Nidesdale, from the head of Kenn to the head of the Water of Cludan, by a dry march; and then by Cludan to its end, wher it runneth into Nith, a mile above Drumfriese; from thence by Nith.

But this fourth part of the Stuartry faileth much from the nature of ane quadrant, for Nithsdale doeth incroach upon its very chord. But, in the first quadrant, the parish of Kirkbeen doeth goe beyond the arch of the quadrant, by its low banks of Arbiglam and Prestoun; and the parish of Minigoff doeth lykewayes extend beyond the arch; as also the parish of Carsfairn. So ballancing the excess of the thrid and first with the want of the fourth, the Stuartry of Kircudbright will be ane hundred miles in circuit.

The part of the Stuartrie that lyeth to the east is very naturally divyded into two parts by the water called Ore, which indeed is the arch of a circle, whose centre is the town of Drumfriese, from which every parte of the water, from the head to the foot, is twelve miles distant.

The water itself, from the head of it, which is the Loch of Ore, partly in the Stuartrie and partly in Niddisdale, to the foot therof, wher it entereth into Sulway Firth at the island called Hestoun, will be twenty miles long, in which are contained ten parishes under the jurisdiction of the Stuart of Kirkcudbright; yett within the diocese of Glasgow, and commissariot of Drumfriese thereunto belonging.

The most northerlie of these parishes is Kirkpatrick Durham, lying upon the Water of Ore. Next to it is the other Kilpatrick, called Irongray, upon the march of Niddisdale. Under Durham, upon the Water of Ore, lyeth the parish of Ore. Eastward from it lyeth Lochrutton. To the east of that is Terreglis, upon the Water of Cludan. Southward, under Terreglis, is Traquire, towards the foot of the river from Drumfriese. Southwards from Ore and Lochrutton, is the parish of Kirkgunzeon. Then upon the Firth of Sulway, betwixt Nith and Ore, from east to west lye orderly, New Abbay, Kirkbein, and Colwen, which is partly on the Firth, and partly on the Water of Ore.

In this part of the shire, to the east of the Loch and Water of Ore, are ye Loughs of Achingibert, Miltoun, Ruttan, Arrturr, Gheerloch, Lochkitt; and the Langwood of Dalskairth. The Earls of Nithsdale are Heritable Stuarts.

The considerable houses are, Kilwhonaty, Edinghaim, Fairgirth, Carguinnan, Drumcayran, Achinskioch, Castel of Wraiths, Drummillem, ye Castle of Terreglis.

The Water of Ore riseth out of Loch Ore, near the head of Niddisdale, and falleth into the Irish Sea twelve myles be east Kirkcuthbright.

The westerne part of this eastern semicircle, which lyeth betwixt the Water of Ore and the higher half of the Water of Kenne, and the lower half of the Water of Dee, containeth eight parishes. The most northerly is Dalry; to the south of that is Balmaclalan; to the south of that is Partoun; to the south of that is Crossmichael, all marching with the two waters except Dalry, which hath a dry march with Niddisdale. Under Crossmichael lyeth Keltoun upon Dee. Eastward from it lyeth Butle upon Ore, whose foresaid arch maketh the nearest distance betwixt the two waters to be only two miles, wheras at the foot it will be twelf. Under these again are

Rerik, marching with Butle on the east, and a bay called Hestoun, within which the Island of Hestoun is, and
on the south with Sulway Firth.   Upon the west is the
parish of Kirk and town of Kircuthbert, which partly
lyeth upon the river, and partly upon the Sulway
Firth.

The towne of Kircudbright lyeth upon the syde of the
river, four miles above the Ross. It hath a commodious
harbour for shipps.   The latitude of the towne of Kir-
cuthbright is 54 gr. 51 m. The longitude may be 19 gr.
Over against the town lyeth the Isle of St Marie, which
maketh the harbour commodious.

The fresh water Loughs in this part of the Stuartrie,
are the Loughs of Fergus, Law Loch, L. Carlingwork,
L. Kon, L. Faldbey, L. Lurkan, L. Erby, L. Corsock,
L. Garchraggan, L. Uuy, the 'Loch of Kenmore,
Loch Trostary, L. Bargatoun, L. Glentow, L. Whymoch,
Lochenbraik, L. Dornel, L. Eiroch, L. Greenoch, L.
Skarrow, L. Fleet, L. Braishuis, L. Forest.

The considerable houses upon the east syde of the
Water of Dee are, Dundrainnan Abbay, Barlocco, Glen-
shinnoch, Orchartoun, Colnachtyr, Lachleir, the Castle
of Treeve, a stronghold belongeth to the King, standeth
in ane island, Balmagy, Kumstoun, Bishoptoun, Plump-
toun, Ainrik, Kelly, Clein, Levistoun, Grenoch, Partoun,
Druymlash, Chirmers, Park, Castle Kenmoir, Trouhain,
Glenly, Barskeoch, Kars, Drumness, Airds, Greenlaw,
Mouwhill, Dungeuch, Banck.

The houses many of them are deckt well with planting.   The considerable woods are upon the west syde of
the Loch of Kenmoir, Karn, Edward Wood, the forest of
Craig Gilbert.

The western semicircle (which marcheth with ye Shyre
of Wigtoun, Carrick, Kyle, and part of Niddesdale) is

most naturally devyded into three parts. The most northerly part thereof is contained betwixt the separate parts of the Water of Kenn and Dee, unto the Loch of Dee; and then the Lane, called the Curine Lane, whose fountaine is within half a myle of the Loch of Dun, and runneth into the Loch of Dee, and then the Loch of Dun and the foresaid dry marches of Kyle and Niddesdale.—This part containeth two vast parishes. The most northerly is Carsefairn. That to the south is the Kells, about a parte of which the Water of Dee and Curine Lane goe lyke the arch of a circle.

The other parte of this western semicircle is notably divided into two by the Water of Fleete, whose fountaine is the Loch of Fleete, within a myle of the Water of Dee, towards its head, and at the foot runneth into the Firth of Cree. The easterne part, betwixt Dee and Fleete, which lyeth to the south of the Kells, containeth five parishes, four whereof lye along the Water of Dee, south one from another orderly, as followeth, viz. Balmacghie, next to Kells; Tungland, next to Balmacghie; Twinam, next to Tungland; next to Twinam, the parish of Borg, lying partly upon the Water and partly upon the Firth of Cree. The fift parish is Girhtowne, lying from the head to the foot of Fleet Water, and marching with all the former four parishes.

The thrid part is contained within the water of Fleet, a part of Dee, the Curine-Lane, thence to Loch-Dun upon the east syde, and upon the south-west and north betwixt the water of Cree and its firth, and the dry march of Carrick to Loch-Dun. And in this thrid part are three parishes, viz. Minigoff, lying to the north, and Kirkmabrike, or Ferritoun, lying to the south upon Cree and its firth, and Anweth, lying to the east of Fer-

ritoun, all along the water of Fleete, from the head to
the foot.

The fresh water Loughs in this part of the Stuartrie
are these Loughs, L. Truyill, L. Vealluy, L. Garony,
Douloch, Loch Dee, L. Middil, Lang Loch, L. Muik,
Sadle Loup L., L. Lilly.

The considerable houses are Kardonesse Castle, Rusko
Castle, Bardarach, Barboom, Karsluith, Kassincary, ye
towne of Ferritoune, Schroinord, Lairg Castle, town of
Minigoff, Gairliss, the residence of the Earle of Galo-
way, Kiste, Cracgnim, Meekledallash, Brygtoun.

The houses in this part of the Stuartrie have many
of ym very much planting about them. Ther be many
woods. The most considerable are the Free Forrest, upon the borders with Kyle, Torchreigan Wood, the Wood
of Gairless, the Wood of Rusco.

OF THE ABBEYS, PRIORIES, AND NUNRIES,

WITHIN THE STEWARTRY OF

KIRKCUDBRIGHT.

Sibbald MSS. Adv. Lib. W. 5. 17.

FIRST, In the parish Terregliss is a great church-
building, called the College. It was a Provestry called
of Lincludan, situate most sweetly in the angle where
Cludan runneth into Nith, a mile above Dumfriess,
built by Queen Margaret, relict of K. James the 4th,
when she was Countess of Douglass.

Secondly, In the parish of New Abbay is an Abbay so

called, and the Abbot thereof was called *Dominus Dulcis*, or my Lord Sweat-heart.

Thirdly, in the parish of Rerik is a large Abbay, called Dundranan, wherein Mr Michael Scott lived.

Fourthly, In the parish of Tungland is the Abbay called Tongland.

Fifthly, In the parish of Galtua (which now, with another called Dunrod, is joyned to the town and parish of Kirkcudbright,) is an island called St Mary, wherein there was a priory, a short mile south and by west from the town, called the Priory of St Mary Isle, one of the most pleasant situations in Scotland.

Sixthly, In the parish of Kirkcrist (which is now annexed to Twiname parish) there was a Nunry, having the lands called Nuntoun and the Nun-Mill thereunto belonging; but now it is scarce known where the Nunry was.

No. III.

DESCRIPTION OF THE PARISH OF KIRKPATRICK DURHAM.

Macfarlane MSS. Vol. I. p. 510.   Adv. Lib. Jac. 5th. 4. 19.

CELLA Patricii, or Kilpatrick of the Moor, called also Kilpatrick Durham, as is reported, because many of that name were in it, though there is none now of that antient stock there, lyes in the Stuartry of Kircudbright, Presbytry and Commissariot of Drumfreis, being on the border of the Presbytry and Commissariot.

1

It is seven miles in length from Bridge of Urr to Blackmark north. Whitenook is also in it; and these two are closs upon Dunscoir, which is in Nithsdale. Eastward of Blackmark Dunscore jetts out somewhat further southward, half a mile or more, for it joins Killpatrick at Mulewell.

Kilpatrick is at any place two miles broade, terminated on the south by Crossmichaell, (in which Achindullie is ;) on the west by Partan, and then by Bamaclellan; on the north by Dunscore, and a very narrow point of Holywood in Nithisdale at Mulewell, where also Irongray touches it, and goes on terminating it on the east; then the paroch of Urr touches it, and crosses the Edin[r] road about a mile or more north of Easter Marwhirn; the paroch of Urr continues to terminate Kilpatrick doun on the east side to the Water of Urr.

Mulewell is of the nature of Merkland Well in Lochrutton, but little resorted to. It lyes on the west of the Edr. road, a mile north of Mule. There is a large stone at it.

The Church of Kilpatrick is nine miles from New Galloway, 13 from Kirkcudbright, 11 miles from Drumfreis, five from Partan Kirk, eight from that of Bamaclellan, twelve from Glencairn, nine from Irongray and Terreglis, and seven large from that of Lochrutton, 4 from Kirkgunzeon, 8 from Cowend, 5 from Butle, 2 from Urr, almost six from Kelton, 3 from Crossmichael.

Kilpatrick Church is distant from Miltoun of Urr three full miles; from Carlingwork, five miles; from Criffell mountain (on the east side of which, near the foot of it, lyes the Church of New Abbay,) 9 miles; from Skreel, a tract of mountains, 7 miles; from Cairnsmuir, a large mountain in Minigaff, running south and north,

18 miles ; from Black Craig of Dunscoir, eight miles ; from Black Craig of Kells, eleven miles ; from Hogghill (on the north-east side of which lyes Terreglis Church) nine miles.

Carlingwork is almost a mile north of Kelton Kirk, and is marked A in the map.

Auchinreach, in Urr, is a large mile from Kilpatrick.

Grange, on Urr, lyes a quarter of a mile below the Bridge of Urr, just on the water almost.

Mollence is not marked in the map. It lyes in Cross Michael, about $\frac{3}{4}$ of a mile from the bridge, a very litle to the east of the meridian line from Kilpatrick Church.

Auchindollie, in Crossmichael, about $1\frac{1}{2}$ miles from Kilpatrick Church.

Glenlair, in Parton, about two miles.

Corsack there, betwixt two and three.

Crogo, in Bamaclellan, about four.

Larg, in Urr, large $2\frac{1}{2}$ mile.

The Rooms that follow are within the Paroch and distant from the Church,   miles.

Bridge of Urr, or Nether Killie Whannedie,	1 large mile.
Over Killie Whannedie,	1 large
Macartney,	$1\frac{1}{2}$
Arkland,	2
Kirklebrids,	$2\frac{1}{4}$
Nether Bar,	3
Over Bar,	4
White Nook,	7
Black Mark,	7
Mule,	$5\frac{1}{2}$
Lochinkit,	almost 4

East Marwhirn,	.	.	. 2
Croketford, .	.	.	. 2½
Barnkylie,	.	.	almost 1
Arimin,	.	.	. 2½

Bennon Hill, 4 large. Its part in Kilpatrick, and part in Irongray.

The Water of Urr, or Orr, comes out of Lochwhirr, about 8 mile and ½ from Kilpatrick Church. A part of Glencairn terminates that Loch on the north; Barnaclelland and Dunscore on the other sides.

The Water of Orr is no large river; it is repute everywher 12 miles distant from Dumfries, but that is not at all exact. It enters the sea, dividing Cowend and Butle.

N.B.—The bearings of the several places above will be known by the map sent herewith. The radius of the circle is a scale of eleven miles.

The way from Edinburgh to Kirkcudbright comes by Penpont, Glencairn, then Girristoun, (about two mile and an half north of Mule,) then to the Mule through the gate, betwixt Mule and Margloly in Irongray; thence south through Kilpatrick Mure, called the Galagate; thence to the Church; thence to Bridge of Urr, to Carlingwork, &c.

From Dumfries to New Galloway ther is a way by Shawhead, Lochinkit, Knock'droket in Nether Bar, near Crogo, Trowhein, &c.

The droves of cattle coming from New Galloway to England come by Trowhen, Knockdroket, then a litle north of Lochinkit till they come to Galagate, and then follow it southward till within about half a mile of Easter Marwhirn, and so on to Larg, and then to Dumfreis, &c.

The best way, but somewhat longer, from Dumfreis to New Galloway, is by Lochruttongate, near the Church,

Miltoun of Urr, Kilpatrick Church, Kilwhanedy, Parton, Shirmers, New Galloway.

From Dumfreis to Kirkcudbright the way is by Miltoun, Grange, Bridge of Urr, Carlingwork, &c. But if the water be litle, the nearer way is by Miltoun Haugh, Carlingwork, &c. This is most patent for coaches and carts, and nearer.

Ther is a Loch in Lochinkit that produces trouts; two small ones in Ariming.

The Black Loch, almost half a mile long, a mile north of the church; a less one, $\frac{1}{4}$ of a mile long, a quarter of a mile from the church, on the west of the Edr. road. These two produce a fish here called Gedds.

There is a Loch of about a mile long that separates Barnkylie and Lairdlouge north of it from Auchinreoch. The road from Dumfreis is $\frac{1}{4}$ mile south of the loch. This Loch hath gedds in it.

The Water of Urr hath salmons and trouts, but not many; hath a stone bridge of two arches at Nether Kelliewhanned; a ruinous timber bridge at Corsack.

About a mile south of Blackmark begins a brook, comes winding down an half quarter of a mile to the east of Over Bar, thence south to Nether Bar, where it turns westward into Urr. It's oft unpassable.

Eastward, about half a mile betwixt Bar and Lochinkit, comes southward from the hills Kirklebride Burn, and when it is a mile below Lochinkit turns westward to the Water of Urr, midway betwixt Kirklebride and Nether Bar. It hath on it a stone bridge of one arch betwixt the Church and Nether Bar.

There is another brook that arises in the mure, runs on the west side of Easter Marwhirn, thence takes a compass westward, and turns eastward again to Barnkylie, which stands just on the brink of it toward Dumfreis.

I

It goes down from Barnkylie, and, without any remarkable turns, enters Urr at Haugh, an half mile above the Church of Urr. Its very rare that this brook is unpassable betwixt Kilpatrick and Dumfreis, even in great rains.

There were Readers in Kilpatrick after the Reformation. The first minister was one Mr Douglass; afterward Mr Adam Brown, deposed Nov. 3, 1656, by the Presbetrie, for a great number of impudencies and reviling his brethren, protesting the Presbytrie were malicious. Mr Gabriel Sempill was ordained there May 26, 1657; turned out, with others, in 1661.

Mr Stark, a very vicious man, succeeded him, and some time after removed to some other place. Mr Alexr. Sangster succeeded, (I know not if immediately,) and continued to the Revolution, when Mr Sempill returned, but was soon transported to Jedburgh. Mr William English was ordained there 1693 or 94; transported to Kilspindy 1698. Mr James Hill was ordained there May 30, 1699.

It hath examinable persons 600 or above; was a mensal-church of the Bishop of Edr., who got 500 merks of the stipend, which is now by decreet of locality bestowed on the minister, the whole being 863 lib. 3s. 4d.

His Majesty now is undoubted patron.

The most part of the paroch is divided into the 50 merk land and 20 pound land. The first is a barony, whereof Nithisdale was superior, and his son is, and proprietor still of a considerable part of it. But this barony paid a few or tack teynd to the Bishop of Edr., now to his Majesty. Its said the twenty pound land belonged to, or held of, the Abbacy of Dundreman; afterward held of, and payed feu to the Bishop of Dunblane. It pays it now to his Majesty.

The most antient and honorable family in the paroch

were the McNaughts of Killwhanned. But that family seems now extinct, the heir of it, a worthy gentleman, by the debts on the fortune, and a liferentrix that eat out the remainder, (being married a 2d time,) being obliged to go to America. This estate held of the King formerly as well as now, and some few others.

Turners Kirkland held formerly of the Abbot of Sweetheart, but now of the Minister, as it did also in the time of Prelacy.

The heritors of any consideration now residing in the paroch are Maxwell of Arkland, and Neilsone of Barnkylie.

The Church of Kilpatrick seems, by an hollow stone fixed in the wall at the church door for holy water, as appears, to have been built in time of Popery. A little steeple was added afterwards; then the isle built in Mr Sempil's time. His sermons were resorted to from other places.

There are the vestiges of an old chappell and churchyard in Ariming. Nothing further is known of it.

Upon the Edr. road a little south of Mule, but within Irongray, is a large stone like a table, on which were placed the elements when Mr John Walsh administered the sacrament there in the time of Prelacy.

About a mile n. from Easter Marwhirn to the east of the Edr. road a litle space, on the east side of Baudsknow, ly interred 4 of these called Whiggs, and ther names incribed on an tombstone. They were found by Captain Bruce and a party of horse; 2 others were wounded, they being six in whole, and hanged next day at Irongray. Bauds-know is within Urr in Larg.

On the 17 day of March yearly is Patrick's mass fair held at the church.

At the Bridge of Urr, within Kilpatrick, there is the

priviledge of a weekly market and a fair the day of the Rood Fair in Dumfreis, and another before the Candlemas Fair there. Others have been much in desuetude, but are now begun to be revived.

Thus I have given an exact account of this paroch, so far as I know, and, for want of more memorable things, inserted some things of small consequence. You may take or omit what you see fitt; you have the true situation of places as to the points and the miles, as commonly reputed to be from Kilpatrick.

No. IV.

DESCRIPTION OF THE PARISH OF MINIGAFF.

Macfarlane MSS. Vol. I. p. 517. Adv. Lib.
Jac. 5th, 4. 19.

THE paroch, as its situate, runs in length from S. to N. for near 15 mile, the Church being situate within 3 mile of the southermost part of it, upon a pleasant rising ground, which overlooks the country for a good distance at the confluence of the river Cree and water of Polkill. The village of Minygaff being situate at the foot of Polkill, in a low ground hard by the Church, there being an artificiall moat, which, by tradition, hath been handed down to posterity, as being at first contrived for sacrifising to Jupiter and the Heathen Gods; and when Christianity obtained, it was used as a mercat-place for the inhabitants to meet and do business, till such time as villages were erected, and places of entertainment prepared, and ale-houses, for converse, intertainment, and interviews.

The river Cree bounds the west side, from its conflux with Polneur water to Lochmoan, from whence it has its rise, (as the minister's description has it, from the furthest extent of this paroch to Lochmoan,) which is the boundary on that quarter; the paroch of Penninghame lying contiguous to it, on the other side of the river, till it is cut out by the paroch of Colmonell up the river.

On the Minigaff side, the Barony of Garlies is extended to the forsaid lake, and gives title to the eldest son of the honourable family of Galloway; and is divided by the water of Minnock, which joyns the river Cree, at a gentleman's seat belonging to a cadet of the family. This small river has its spring in the Baloch mountains, continuing its course till it comes here; running through the midle of that Barony, till it is cut out on the east side by the small water of Troul, which is a boundary on the west side of the Barony of the Forrest, belonging to John M'Kye of Palgown, in which stands the famous mountain of the Mearock, which overlooks all the other mountains for hight; on the east side whereof, are the lakes of Lochenoch, Lochnildricken, and Lochwachlan, and has its boundary on the north; the paroch of Collmonel, (Cammonel,) and Straiton, on the east; Corsfairn paroch and the Kells being a ground wholly fitt for pasturage.

This Barony of the Forrest, or Buchan, has on the south the Loch of Troul, where the said Palgown has a seat, overlooked by a mountain, on the north, betwixt which and the lake, the house is very pleasantly seated; the lake appearing like a large pond under the house, well stocked with pikes; there being a prodigious num-

ber of large oak-trees (all lying across one another)
lying in its bottom, that within the opposite mountains
on the other side, one would be astonished (in a clear
day) to think where they came from.

The house is surrounded with pretty groves of Scots
pines, black cherries, and other kinds of planting, which
make a fine umbello to the house ; and from the front, a
walk down to the lake, which centers upon a little mote,
prettily planted in devices with seats, and a beautifull
litle boat, lodg'd ther under a shade, for taking pleasure
in a fine day upon the water.

This Barony produces the best sheep of any part of
this paroch, and sold in the mercats at very good prices ;
and so inclosed and divided, for the orderly improvment
of the sheep and black cattle, that the whole farmers of
these grounds have considerable advantage therby, to
the inriching of ther families. In the remote parts of
this great mountain, are very large Red-deer ; and about
the top thereof, that fine bird, called the Mountain Par-
tridge, or, by the commonalty, the Tarmachan, about
the size of a Red-cock, and its flesh much of the same
nature ; feeds, as that bird doth, on the seeds of the
bullrush, and makes its protection in the chinks and
hollow places of thick stones, from the insults of the
eagles, which are in plenty, both the large gray and the
black, about that mountain.

On the south side of this lake joyns the Barony of
Garlies, and takes up a long extent of ground, most part
mountainous, and is confined by Heron, of that ilk, his
ground on the north-east part, and then by the water of
Polkill, which has its spring in these mountains, running
four or five miles, till it joyns with the Cree River, near
the Church of Minigaff, a small ground of Herons (viz.

the artificial Mote spoke of above) lying betwixt it and the church.

In the Barony of Garlies is a very large extent of ground, all very fitt for pasturage; having on the Cree side a very long tract of fine wood, growing along the side of the river, where it forms itself into a lake, called the Loch of Cree; at the head of which there is a famous house, of a most beautifull situation, occasioned by the islands in that lake, and garnishing of woods on each side; and on the river, the Earl has a leap for salmond, and a corn-milne, having no other heritors' estate mixing with it; but only ane gentleman of the name of M'Kie, a cadet of the family of Palgown, called Doncaird, whose lands ly on the water of Minnock.

On the other side of the Barony of Garlies, lyes the antient seat of the Stewarts of Gairlies. They were antiently called Thanes of Dalswinton, before they got this Barony by a gift from the King, before the Soveraign advanced them to the dignity of nobility.

And it is to be remembred, at a house called the Caldons, that remarkable scuffle hapned between the mountaniers and Coll Douglas, at which time Captain Orchar (I think it should be Urquhart) was killed: there was one particular worth the noticing, that, when two of these people were attacked, they got behind the stonedyke, with their pieces cocked for their defence. Upon their coming up at them, marching very unconcernedly, one of their peices went off, and killed Captain Orchar dead; the other peice designed against Douglas wou'd not go off, nor fire, for all the man could do, by which the Coll., afterwards General Douglas, escaped the danger.

There were six of the mountaneers killed, and no more

of the King's forces but one dragoon. One of these poor
people escaped very wonderfully, of the name of Dinn or
Dun : two of the dragoons pursued him so closely, that
he saw no way for escape ; but at last flying in towards
the lake, the top of a little hill intercepted the soldiers'
view, he immediately did drop into the water all, under
the brae of the lake, but the head, a heath-bush covering
his head, where he got breath ; the pursuer cryed out,
when he could not find him, that the devil had taken him
away.   That morning Captain Orchar had that expression, that, being so angry with the badness of the way,
he wished the devil might make his ribs a broiling-iron
to his soul, if he should not be revenged on the Whiggs
that day, which was the Sabbath morning, he entred the
Glen of Troul, and according to his wish, came upon
these poor people, as they were worshiping God upon his
day, with a surprizing crueltie.

The church in this paroch stands most pleasantly on
a rising ground, where Cree and Polkill meet, command-
ing a pleasant prospect to the sea. Along the river, being invironed with Heron's land, and at the bottom of
this rising ground, on the east side of Polkill, stands the
village of Minnigaff, with a handsome, now ruinous
house, overlooking the village ; near to which stands
Heron's house, upon a rising ground, with a prospect to
the sea, and overlooks a great part of the adjacent country ; his lands extending eastward for two myles, and
then bounded by the water of Palneur, reaching alongst
it, near to three miles ; the lands nearest it being all
covered with woods, with fine openings of medow grounds
and corn-fields ; as ye goe along it, the ground, next
Heron's house, being all devided and adorned with large
thickets of fir and other planting.

At the foot of his avenue, is that large and pleasant plain, called the Green of Machirmore, where that famous battle, betwixt the Romans and Pick, confederates on one side, and the Scots on the other, was fought. *Vide* Buchan. *in Vita Eugenii primi;* the author of the manuscript gives the whole.

Mr Heron, one day making pitts for a plantation of firs in that plain, was persuaded by a friend standing by him, to open a large mount of earth standing in the midle of the ground, and to take the old earth to put into the pitts to encourage his trees to take, and upon the opening of it, found it to be a Roman urn. The top of the mount was all covered over with a strong clay, half yard deep, under which there was half a yard deep of gray ashes, and under that there was an inch thick of a scurff like mug mettall, bran-colour'd, which took a stroak of the pick-ax to break it, under which the workmen found a double wall, built circular-ways, about a yard deep, full of red ashes, like those of a great furnace. When these were taken out, at the bottom there was a large flagstone, six foot long, and three broad, covering a pitt of a yard deepth; and when they hoised up the stone, they observed the bones of a large man lying entire; but when they struck upon the stone to break it, they fell down in ashes; ther was nothing more found in it. There is above a dozen of great heaps of stones detached over the plain, in which were found several urns; but none so memorable as this. And where the Scots got that finishing-stroak at Lochdoon, there is a prodigious Cairn erected, all of gathered stones to cover the dead.

Half a mile from Heron's house eastwards, stands the ruins of the old seat of the M'Kies of Larg, one of the three families of Comloddan, founded by K. Rob. Bruce, at the conclusion of his wars, as ye shall hear hereafter, now in Heron's possession, and has a good salmond-fishing on the water of Cree.

Down the river, about a mile from the Church, lye the lands belonging to Dunbar of Machermore, who has a very agreable seat and a castle standing pleasantly upon the river, with a large plott of fine fir-planting, overlooking a rich ink ground, that lyes twixt the castle and the river, with a good salmond-fishing. His estate, for the most part, lying along the east side of river Cree[1] (which there imitates the windings of the river Forth, and the ground that of the Carse of Stirling,) for two miles, until it terminates upon the water of Polneur, where it unites with Cree, and on the north (and east) with Heron's land.

From the Church north-east, lye the lands of Murdoch of Camloddan, beginning at the bridge of Polkill, one-fourth of a mile above the church, and running along the east side of that water, till it come where Polkill takes its rise ; and is situate 'twixt that and Polneur, all the way on the west side of the last water, till it comes to Tonotrie, a ground of Machirmore's, in which there is some lead found, but in no great quantity. Which house keeps a change (the publick road to Edinburgh and Glasgow passing that way) with another change-house, further on that water, belonging to Heron, called Craigdens, by which ther is a beautifull cascade, as is to be seen in the country, being a large fall of water, as it were out of a tunnell, fourteen foot high, into a prodigious large bason, which causeth a murmuring noise at a great distance ; and over the cascade is a very high rock, covered over with variety of evergreens, and other shrubs, all

---

[1] Here are spirlings, nowhere else to be found but in Forth.

overlooking the cascade, which makes the place very cool, and a very desirable amusement to the curious.

This gentleman's ground is likewise devided by a ground of Heron's, called Drighmirn and Polnie, by a brook, till ye come to Lochdie, which is a place where the water of Die takes its beginning ; and on the top of Polnie mountain, there is a famous deep lake, of good extent, well stocked with salmond-trouts.

Mr Murdoch's seat stands about two mile off the Church, upon the water of Polkill, in a wood, with a good house and orchards, with a leap for catching of fish, naturally in a rock, which goes through the water. His estate is all good pasture-ground. This is the only family that exists (if it may be said to exist, when the estate is sold, and the gentleman bankrupt) of the three brothers, who were honored by K. Rob. Bruce to be proprietors of the thirty pound land of Comloddon ; the manner they acquired it was this :—

King Robert, being by a part of the English army defeat in Carick, fled into the head of Lochdie to a few of his broken partie, and lodging in a widow's house, in Craigencallie, in the morning she, observing some of his princely ornaments, suspected him to be a person of eminence, and modestly asked him in the morning, if he was her Leidge Lord. He told her Yes, and was come to pay her a visit ; and asked her if she had any sons to serve him in his distress. Her answer was, that she had three sons to three severall husbands ; and that if she was confirmed in the truth of his being their sovereign, they should be at his service. He askt her farther, if she could give him anything to eat. Her answer was, there was litle in the house, but agust meal and goats'-milk, which shou'd be prepared for him ; and while it was making ready, her three sons did appear, all lusty men.

The King askt them, if they wou'd chearfully engage in his service, which they willingly assented to; and when the King had done eating, he askt them what weapons they had, and if they could use them; they told him they were used to none but bow and arrow. So, as the King went out to see what was become of his followers, all being beat from him but 300 men, who had lodged that night in a neighbouring glen, he askt them if they could make use of their bows. M'Kie, the eldest son, let fly an arrow at two ravens, parching upon the pinacle of a rock above the house, and shot them through both their heads. At which the King smiled, saying, I would not wish he aimed at him. Murdoch, the second son, let fly at one upon the wing, and shot him through the body; but M'Lurg, the third son, had not so good success.

In the meantime, the English, upon the pursuit of K. Robert, were incamped in Moss Raploch, a great flow on the other side of Die. The King observing them, makes the young men understand that his forces were much inferior. Upon which they advised the King to a stratagem, that they would gather all the horses, wild and tame, in the neighbourhood, with all the goats that cou'd be found, and let them be surrounded and keept all in a body by his soldiers in the afternoon of the day, which accordingly was done. The neighing of the horses, with the horns of the goats, made the English, at so great a distance, apprehend them to be a great army, so durst not venture out of their camp that night; and by the break of day, the King, with his small army, attacked them with such fury, that they fled precipitantly, a great number being killed; and ther is a very big stone in the center of the flow, which is called the King's Stone to this day, to which he leaned his back, till his men gather'd up the spoil; and within these thirty yeares, there were broken swords and heads of picks got in the flow, as they were digging out peats.

The three young men followed closs to him in all his wars to the English, in which he was successfull, that at last they were all turn'd out of the kingdom, and marches established 'twixt the two nations; and the soldiers and officers that followed him were put in possession of what lands were in the English hands, according to their merite. The three brothers, who had stuck closs to the King's interest, and followed him through all dangers, being askt by the King, what reward they expected? answered very modestly, That they never had a prospect of great things; but if his Majesty would bestow upon them the thirty pound land of the Hassock and Comloddan, they would be very thankfull; to which the King chearfully assented, and they kept it long in possession.

The line of M'Lurg's first failing in are male, matched with one Captain Heron, a second brothir of Sir Cuthbert Heron of Chipchase, in Northumberland, and was called Comloddan Heron M'Lurg till this day. The M'Donals of Fisgaill broke in at last upon a part of the estate, upon which Peter built the Castle of Machermore. It went from him to a cadet of the Dunbars of Entriken.

[M. D. says nothing of Heron's marying the heiress of M'Clurg, only that it failed first, and went into the hands of the M'Donals, who kept it a long time, and says the eldest brother's family is now in a great measure extinct, only that branch remaining of the M'Kies of Palgoun. The estate of Larg is now in the possession of Heron of that ilk.]

Murdoch, the second brother, is the only family that has continued in the name lineally. The eldest assumed for coat of arms, two ravens proper upon a chief argent, with an arrow through both their heads, gules, the field gules. Murdoch carrys argent on a chief gules, a raven volant proper, with an arrow through his body. Of the second, the farthest extent of this gentleman's estate terminates upon Lochdie, from whence the water of Die runs, being a great lake full of pyks, and ane excellent fish, called a salmond-trout, being red in the fish, and the sides all enamuled with red spots.

The lowest part of the paroch is now in possession of David Maxwell, son to Coll. William Maxwell of Cardiness, and Andrew Heron of Burgally, (author of this description, but is now dead.) That which has its termination upon Girthon and Kirkmabrieck belongs to Mr Maxwell, being a small barony, called Bardrochwood, lying on the water of Polneur, near to whose foot is a bridge of one arch, all garnished with wood for a mile alongst the river, and had a little convenient house upon it, now in ruines ; but Mr Maxwell has built at Greddock, three miles south of the Church, a pretty little house and garden ; his land extends to the top of Cairnsmuire mountain, all good pasture, and some corn-land.

Burgally, the possession of Mr Heron, lyes south of the Church two miles and half; above these lands, closs upon the river for a mile and half, most part whereof is garnished with wood, alongst the river, of a considerable value. The land extends to Cairnsmure, whereunto the greatest part of that mountain belongs, where there is good store of Bristol stone of divers colours, very well cutt naturally; very large Red-deer, with plenty of mountain Patridges, and other muir-fowl; having a convenient litle house upon the water-side, with orchards, and other amusements very agreeable to a country gentleman ; with great variety of excellent fruits, of all kinds the climate will produce; and a great many evergreens, both foreign and exotick. [I suppose he means domestick; but the minister's description, designed for Mr Maitland, and which is a very incorrect copy of Bargallys, has it exotick.]

Our present minister is Mr Thomas Campbell, who maried a sister of Murdoch of Comloddan, now deceast; he has by her severall sons and daughters.

Thus far Andrew Heron of Bargally, Esquire, uncle to the present Heron of that ilk, who is now in possession of that estate.

What follows is added by the minister to be sent to Mr Maitland.

The paroch of Minigaff lyes in the County of Galloway, and Stewartry of Kirkcudbright, divided from the Shire of Galloway by the river Cree; some of the head of the paroch is bounded by Carrick, in Ayrshire. The catechisable persons are about 900. The King is patron of the paroch.

The minister's stipend is about   merks Scots, which is paid mostly by the heritors. The manse was built a few years ago, and the gleeb is both little and bad. The church, lately repaired, is a long edifice from east to west, and neither in it, or the church-yard, are there any monuments worth notice. [There are some stones, on the two gates of the church-yard, with some proper inscriptions from the Psalms, and a dyal in the midle of the church-yard, all done with Bargally's own hand; but by the by he is not buried here, for he erected a stately tomb in his own garden, some years before his death, with his own and lady's arms, and other decorements, where they both are buried.]

The greatest part of the paroch is mountainous, and

so fittest for pasturage ; but what cultivate, and much more might be cultivate, produces very good grain ; but black cattle and sheep are the produce of the country, on which they, in Shire and Stewartry, live more plentifully than any communality in Scotland, having alwise flesh once a day. Their fewall is peats, turff, and wood. There are no remarkable harbours, though ships of fifty or sixty tuns may come up to Machermore.

No. V.

DESCRIPTION OF THE SHERIFFDOM OF WIGTOUN, BY SIR ANDREW AGNEW OF LOCHNAW, AND DAVID DUMBAR OF BALDOON ; ENLARGED BY SIR ROBERT SIBBALD.

Description of Scotland. Sibbald MSS. Adv. Lib. Jac. 5th. 1. 4.

THE Sherifdome of Wigtoun is named from Wigtoun, the head towne thereof.

It hath upon the east and south the Stewartrie of Kirkcudbright, and is devyded therfra by ane ferry of four myle in breadth, called the Water of Cree, which is of that breadth twelf myles up ; and from that ferry northward up, the said water of Cree is the march. The Bailerie of Carrick, within the Sherifdome of Air, boundeth the said Shyre of Wigtoun on the north, and upon the west, with the Irish sea, and it bounds upon the south be the sea which is betwixt Scotland and the Isle of Man.

1

The length of this Shyre is, from the Mule of Galloway to the water of Cree, thirty myle, and fra the Isle of Quhithorne to the Rowntree Burn thirty mile, being the breadth of the same. Some think the greatest breadth will be but twenty-six miles.

That part of the Shyre which lyeth to the west of Luss river, is called the Rine or Snout of Galloway, and the outmost point of it is called the Mule.

The principall rivers within the Shyre are, first, the river of Cree, which devides the Shyre from the Stewartrie. This river of Cree hath its rise in Carrick, where it bordereth with this Shyre. It runneth from the north to the south, through the lough of Cree, and falleth into the sea, in the Bay of Wigtoun. It aboundeth with salmond and spirlings.

The next river is Blaidzenoch, which floweth from the montanous parts of Penningham, and runs fra the north to the south. It runeth through Lochmabary, (wherin ther is ane litle isle, with ane house upon it,) and by the way it receaveth into it severall waters; the most considerable is the water of Tarfe, which hath its rise from Airtfeeld, in the Muirs of Luce, and falleth into Blaidzenoch, under the house of Craighlaw. Then Blaidzenoch turns to the east, and after it heth fra its source run twenty miles, it falleth into the Bay of Wigtoun, near above the place of Baldone.

The water of Malzie ryseth out of the Lough of Mochrom, and passeth the Castle of Mochrom, and runs from the south to the north-east, and runs by Cree Loch; and after it heth runn some five miles, it entereth the Blaidzenoch below Dalrugle.

The water of Luce riseth upon the march with Carrick, and runeth much in a streight lyne from north to

K

south, devyding the Shyre in two. It runneth some twelfe myles, and doeth receave into it severall waters; the most considerable is the Croce Water, which flowes from Airtfield, and runs six miles, and passing the Lairg, runs into Luss at the Muir-kirk. Upon this water of Luss, and the bay of it, lyeth the Regality of Glenluce; and a myle or so above it, upon the water of Luss, stands the Abbay of Glenluss. This Bay of Glenluss is by Ptolomee called *Rerengonius Sinus*, and this bay runing in upon the east syde of the Mule, unto the Abbey of Glenluce, with Loch Rian, which from the north runneth in upon the west syde, forme the peninsul called the Rine, the neck of land betwixt them being three or four myle broad.

The water of Solburn floweth from Lough Connoll, and runneth four myle, and then falls into Loch Ryane.

Poltantoun water flowing from Auchnatroch, and runs eight miles, ere it fall in the sea at Luce, two myle below Garthland Castle.

The two salt loughs of Loch Ryan and Luce invirone the Presbiterie of Stranraar, and make it a peninsula. Stranrawer stands at the south end of the lough, and about two myle to the east stands the town of Innermessan.

Loch Rian runs in the land ten myle from the North sea, and stoppeth betwixt Innermessan and Stranraar.

Luss Lough runs fra the Mule of Galloway to the Craigs of Craignargat, sixteen myles, wher it stopps upon the Muchrom shore, in the mouth wherof ther lyeth three rocks, called Bigiskarris.

It is said ther is a place of the sea, close upon the Mule, wher ships, if they enter, are quickly turned round and sunk down.

The ports upon this parte of the Shyre are Portpatrick, wher, upon a litle bay, stands the town and harbour; it being very near to Ireland, is the common passage thither. Near to it, close by the sea, is a cave, called the Cave of Uchtriemackean, accessible by six steps of a stair, entering to a gate built with stone and lime, at the end of which is a structur lyke ane altar. The people frequent this place the first night of May, and wash deseased children with the water, which runs from a spring over the cave.

Port Montgomerie.

Lough Ryan.

The most considerable fresh-water lochs, in the Presbitery of Stranraar, are the Lough of Dalskilpin, ane myle in length, and half a mile broad.

The Loughs of Inchcrinnell, and Inch, wherin stands ane tour, called Castle Kenedie, belonging to the Earl of Cassills. The Loch of Saltside, upon which the Abbacie stands. The Loch of Lochnaw, wherin the Kings of old had ane house. Near to it stands the house of Lochnaw, the residence of the Heritable Sheriff of Wigtoun.

The principal houses in this parte of the Shyre, are Drummour, Logan, Arduall, Killesser, Balgregan, Clonyeart, Garthland, Dunskey, Lochnaw, Corswall, Glaidsnoch, Chappell, Castle Kenedie, Innermessan, Craigcaffie, Park, Synoness, Carscreoch. [Glasserton, the Earl of Galloway's seat; Castle Keneday, Earl of Stair's; Garthland, Mackdougall's; Lochnaw, Colonel Agnews; Revenston, William Stuart's of Castle-Stuart; Sorbie, Colonel James Stuart's. Agnew of Lochnaw is Hereditarie Sheriff.] [1]

The other part of the Shyre, which makes the Pres-

---

[1] The passage within brackets has been supplied in the original Manuscript by a later hand.

biterie of Wigtoun, heth in it the Bay, or loch of salt-water, of Wigtoun, that will be four myles broad, and eight in length. Ther is ane bank of shells upon it, that furnisheth the countrey with lyme, which they make with peits. This bank of shells is observed not to diminish.

. Upon this bay, betwixt the mouth of Cree, and of the river Bladnoch, is situat the town of Wigtoun, which giveth title to the Chief of the Flemings, who were ancient lords, and now are Earls of Wigtoun. It is a Burgh Royall, and the head of the Shyre. It heth ane good harbourie. Near to it is the Monument of the King Galdus, (from whom some think the Shyre was named.) Ther is ther ane large circle of ground, set round with long obelisk stones, and some shorter ones in the middle.

Some five or six miles to the south of this, stands the Royall Burgh of Whithern, wher stands the Priorie. It is the Bishop seat, and the Isle of Whithern makes a port to it.

The fresh-water lochs in this district are Aplebie **L.**, ane myle long, and half a myle broad; Ravenston L. of the same quantity; the **Whyt L.** of Myrtoun, which never freeseth, wheron the **Laird of Mairton's** house standeth; the L. of Mochram, wheron stands the house of Mochram, which L. aboundeth with Herons and wild Geese; the L. of Uchiltrie, Lochmaberie, and Lochcronal.

Ther are, in this part of the Shyre, of considerable houses, the Castells of Phisgill, Iyll, Glassertoun, Wig, Ravinstoun, Crugletoun, Mairtoun, Barinbaro, Brughtoun, Baldoon, Torhouse, Grainge, Craiglaw, Mochrome, Castle-Stuart, Cleray.

The houses are generally dect with planting; but the wood considerable, is the wood of Cree.

The Abbacies, in this Shyre, are these of Glenluce and Saulseate.

No. VI.

Further Account anent Galloway, by Dr Archbald.

Sibbald MSS. Adv. Lib. W. 5. 17.

Sea Fishes in Galloway.

A Bayin, a thick little fish, about a foot long, red coloured, with some white spots in the belly, narrow tailed, with an hard small head; a very well-tasted fish, but full of small bones like a pike.

A Lyth, about the bigness of a small salmon-gilse, not unlike in shape, but dark-gray coloured; it's esteemed the best fish in all the coast.

A Blockan, about the bigness of a white salmond-trout, of shape and colour like the lyth, but a dryer fish.

Dog-fish, about the length of a little salmon, but smaller of body, big-headed, hollow-eyed; but draws very narrow at the tail, with a stiff thick fin, of a silver-gray colour. His skin is so rough, that no man is able to draw one of them over his shoulders, the skin takes such hold of his clothes. They do not spawn as other fishes, but ferries the young at the navel, which I frequently saw, after they were catched. Their fish is not good.

The Sand-eel is of the shape of a fresh-water eel, about a foot or some more in length, but very clear, almost transparent. They are catched in the sand at low tide, and well tasted; they are catchable with angle at the sea-shore.

The Pillock is a large fish, about ten foot long, and as great of body as ane ordinare horse, almost shaped like a pike, black coloured, with a long head, and a monstrous number of teeth, all of equal length. It is seldom catched but when inveigled in herring-nets. The countrey people make oyl of them.

Fresh-Water Fishes there.

A Nembling-skeal, shaped like a herring, but of the quantity of a salmond-gilse, with scales so hard, that it is hardly penetrable; and when it comes up the river, it affrights all other fishes, so that the fishing proves alwayes bad, when they abound.

The Horn-eel, about two foot long, not far from the shape of another eel. It hath a pike out of its forehead, like the figured horn of an unicorn, coloured like a spurling, and eatable.

The Conger-eel is of length more than twelve foot; the skin of it is very strong, which the inhabitants make use of for girths to their horses, lasting very long.

A Brandling is a little fish, found in the water of Fleit, about the bigness of a little trout, with many red spots, but very excellent fish; where also are found pearls.

A Cuddin is a little fish, as big as a large trout, short but thick-bodied; its belly a pure red colour; its tast very sweet; and is only found in a lake, called Lake Grenoch, in a very wild moorish place, where they abound.

There is a large cave, called the Cave of Uchtrie Macken, close by the sea, near Portpatrick, accessible by six steps of a stair, entering a gate built with stone and lime; at the end of which is built an altar, at least a structure after that figure, to which many people resort upon the first night of May, and there do wash deseased children with water, which runs from a spring over the cave, and afterwards they ty a farthing, or the like, and throw it upon the altar.

There is a well, called Kernadert, in the parish of the Callis. The water is very sweet, to which many people resort, who are distempered with sore heads or stomachs, and it proves effectuall.

As for other wells then these which I formerly mentioned, savouring of Moffet wells, they are only used superstitiously, and their usefullness seeming fabulous, they are not worthy to trouble you with their names.

There is a little isle beside the Mule of Galloway, where, if sheep shall feed but a little, their teeth are immediately gilded of a golden colour.

There is a place of the sea, close upon the Mule, where ships, if they enter, are quickly turned round and sunk down. Whether it be from contrary tides or a catadup, I know not; but I am informed of it by the Laird of Mule living there.

No. VII.

THE following account of the Presbytery of Penpont was drawn up and transmitted to Sir Robert Sibbald, by the Rev. Mr Black, minister of Closeburn. It contains a variety of curious historical notices, and forms a very suitable appendix to a volume of Gallovidian Statistics.

A Briefe Description of the Bounds of the Presbytery of Penpont, being the upper Part of the Sheriffdom of Nidesdale.

Sibbald MSS. Adv. Lib. W. 5. 17.

NIDESDALE is called by Buchanan *Nithia, a Nitho amne,* which river doth run out of a small fountain, near Damellintoun, in Kyle, out of a hill, called   ,
and runneth in a small rivulet for several miles, until it come to Castle of Cumlock; and waxing greater and greater by receiving other rivers, doth run a course of above thirty miles, dividing the Sheriffdom all along to the Colledge of Lincluden, in the Stewartry of Galloway, near to the town of Dumfreiss, where receiving a little water, called Cludan, it divides Nidesdale from the lower part of Galloway, called the Stewartry of Kirkcudbright, and running by the parishes of Terregles, Traquare, New Abbay, and Kirbeen, on the Galloway side, and by the town and parish of Drumfreiss, and Carlaverock, on the Nidesdale side, it doth empty itself in the English sea, or Solway Firth, a little beneath the Castle of Carlaverock, in Nidesdale, and beneath the great hill called Chriffell, in Galloway.

Nidesdale is joyned with Annandale in the election of Commissioners for the Parliament; and the Barons of both are indifferently elected; but is in jurisdiction separated from it, Annandale being a Stewartry having a jurisdiction by itself; but Nidesdale is a Sheriffdom, where my Lord D. of Queensberry, his Majestie's High Treasurer, is Heritable Sheriff. But the jurisdiction of the Sheriff here is not considerable, partly for that the interest of the Duke is interwoven in many of the parishes, and there be some whole parishes belonging to his Grace, whereby his whole interest, being a Regality, is subject to his Baillie ; and partly for that there are several Baronies in this Shire, all which are subject to the jurisdiction of their immediate superiours.

The whole churches of the Sheriffdom of Nidesdale and Stewartry of Annandale being four Presbyteries, did constitute one Provincial Synod, untill the late restitution of Episcopacy; but since that time, all the four Presbyteries are within the Diocese of Glasgow.

The Militia of Nithesdale and Annandale, consisting of a considerable regiment of foot, and a troup of horse ; the Duke of Queensberry is Collonell to the foot, and his Grace's son, the E. of Drumlanrig, is Rootmaster to the horse.

But as to the Presbytery of Penpont ; beginning at the head of the river, the first parish is Kirkconnall, so denominated from *Sanctus Convallus*, who lived in a cell by the vestiges of its foundation, yet perceptible, hard by the fountain he did usually drink of, called *Fons Convalli*, or St Conall's Well, at the foot of an hill, where Kirkconall Church is situate. This parish hath on the south-west side the parish of Cumlock, in Kyle, where is the hill of Corsencon, the march between Kyle and Nidesdale ; and on the west side, a part of the parish of Afleck, in Kyle. This parish lyeth on both sides of the river of Nith, and on the south side marcheth with the parish of Corsfairn, in Galloway ; and on the south-east side, is divided from the parish of Sanquhar by a rivulet called Killo ; on the south side of Nith, and on the east side, from the forenamed parish of Sanquhar, by a little water, called Crawick ; and on the north and north-west side, it is divided from the parishes of Douglass and Crawford-John, in Clidesdale.

In the upper part of this parish, there hath been a Convent, or Religious House, near to the Church, called Karko, afterward the dwelling-house of a family of the name of Crichtoun, whose title it was. They say also, that there hath been in this parish a Nunry. The whole parish belongeth now to my Lord D. of Queensberry, who is patron of the Church. The ground is tolerably fruitfull, both for corn and cattel, and in many places well stored with coal. There is one coal-pit, called Parbrock, which, as is thought, was first begun to be wrought out by the Picts, whose pillars, curiously wrought, are yet to be seen. It is an excellent one, which they are working out at this day. There is no more work in any other place, except in the brinks of some burns, there are some coals picked out by the countrey-men. The grain here is oats and some barley.

The next parish is that of Sanquhar, so denominated from *Sanctus Quarus*, who lived here, which, lying on both sides of the river Nith, as the former, is divided from Kirkconnal by the water of Killo, on the south-west and south side of Nith ; and on the north side of the water, by the river of Crawick on the west side ; and on the north side, from the parish of Crawford-John, in Clidesdale ; and on the east side, it is divided from the parish of Kirkbride by an impetuous water, called Menock. Upon the north side of Nith, near to the water of Crawick, stands the Church of Sanquhar, a considerable and large fabrick, consisting of a spacious church and a stately quire, where are the tombs of severall of the Lord Crichtons of Sanquhar, wrought in free-stone, and before them some Lords of the name of Ross. Near to the Church is situate the town of Sanquhar, a Burgh Royall of old, and having as yet a Commissioner in the Parliament ; a weekly mercat and some fairs in the year. It was made a Gild City in the reign of K. James the Sixth. It hath no great trade or resort unto it, partly by reason of its great distance from the sea, and partly because the inhabitants about it are but few. In old times the citizens were stout men, who, with assistance of their neighbours of the parish without the burgh, made usually an effectual resistance to the Borderers, making inrodes for prey in a part of this parish, and oftentimes pursued them with loss, though their numbers were considerable. A little beneath the Burgh stands the Castle of Sanquhar, a stately edifice, strongly built, which belonged formerly to the Lord Sanquhar, now E. of Dumfreiss; but now the said Castle, with all the lands of the parish, on the north side of the river, except the Burrow lands, and the greatest part of the lands upon the south side, doth belong in property to the D. of Queensberry, except the Barony of Elleock, whereunto the Duke is superiour. It belongs to the E. of Carnwath in property, having the mansion-place Elleock situate in the bounds of it; a goodly fabrick, formerly the dwelling-place of the Barons of Dalyell, of which the Earles of Carnwath are descended. This part of the parish is exceedingly well stored with wood; but now of late, by the cutting down of a great part of it, for the lead-mines of Hopetown, in Clidesdale, and not parking of it afterwards, it is much decayed, and probably will decay more, if, after the cutting of it, it be not more carefully inclosed for the future. In this parish of Sanquhar is coal on both sides of the river; and on the north side of the parish, near to Clidesdale, there is a lead-mine of excellent fine lead, in a place pertaining to the D. of Queensberry, called Cumlock, which was begun to be wrought out in the reign of K. James the Fifth, and afterward intermitted; but of late hath begun to be wrought, and is now a-working out. Near to the Castle of Sanquhar, there are several parks on both sides of the river, one whereof is well stored with deer and other animals that are for pleasure, and others for cattle and these that are for profit; both are like to abound further in time.

One remarkable particular is not to be here omitted. In the year 1653, when the loyal party did arise in arms against the English in the West and North Highlands, some noblemen and loyall gentlemen, with others, were forward to repair to them with such parties as they could make, which the English, with marvelous diligence night and day, did bestir themselves to impede, by making their troups of horse and dragoons to pursue the loyal party in all places, that they might not come to such a considerable number as was designed. It happened one night that one Captain Mason, commander of a troup of dragoons that came from Carlisle, in England, marching through the town of Sanquhar in the night, was in the town of Sanquhar encountred by one Captain Palmer, commander of a troup of horse that came from Air, marching eastward, and meeting at the town-house or tolbooth, one David Veitch, brother to the Laird of Dawick, in Tweddale, and one of the loyall party, being prisoner in irons by the English, did arise, and came to the window at their meeting, and cryed out, that they should fight valiantly for K. Charles; wherethrough they, taking each other for the loyall party, did begin a brisk fight, which continued for a while, till the dragoons having spent their shot, and finding the horsemen to be too strong for them, did give ground; but yet retired in some order toward the Castle of Sanquhar, being hotly pursued by the troup through the whole town, above a quarter of a mile, till they came to the Castle where both parties did, to their mutual grief, become sensible of their mistake. In this skirmish there were several killed on both sides, and Captain Palmer himself dangerously wounded, with many mo wounded in each troup, who did peaceably dwell together afterward for a time, until their wounds were cured in Sanquhar Castle.

The third parish is Kirkbride, lying also on both sides of the river, as the two forementioned. It is divided from Sanquhar, on the west part of it, by the impetuous rivulet Menock, on the north side, and by the burn or rivulet of   , on the south side of Nith, and by another rivulet or burn, called Enterkin, it is divided from the parish of Dursdeer on the east side; as also on the south side, it is divided from the same parish of Dursdeer; and on the north side, from the parish of Crawford Lindsay, in Clidesdale, by the hills at Enterkin-head. It is but a little parish, of a small rent, and few inhabitants. The Church is but a little fabrick, at the donation of the D. of Queensberry. The Church is denominate from St Brigid. Here dwelt formerly the Lairds of Cosshowgell of the name of Douglass, and the Lairds of Mackmath of Ahensow. But these linages being now extinct, the whole parish pertains to the D. of Queensberry. There is one monument in the Church of one John of Rockell, with this inscription, *Hic situs est Joannes de Rockell, Jurisconsultus Ecclesiæ*. In the rivulets that flow down from the hills of this parish, is great store of trouts, which, though they fal down by great precipices and rocks, in the way to the river, so that they cannot get up again; yet in the upper ground, there is plenty of them, that they yearly spawn great numbers.

The fourth parish is that of Dursdeer, lying upon both sides of the river Nith, as the three former. It is divided on the west side by Enterkin Burn, as is said; on the

north side of Nith, and on the south side from Penpont;
on the south side of Nith, by a burn called   ;
on the east side from Penpont, also by the Tibber's burn,
otherwise called the Park Burn, near to Drumlanrig;
and on the north side of Nith, it is divided from the parish of Morton, on the north-east side, by the water of
Carren; and on the north-west side, from Crawford
Lindsay, in Clidesdale, by the hill of Loders, and other
places eastward. On the north side of this parish stands
the mansion-place of Dalvine, formerly belonging to a
linage of the name of Douglass, descended from the E.
of Douglass; but that linage being now extinct, the
whole interest of that family pertains to the D. of
Queensberry. The house is situate in a pass betwixt
two hills, near to Crawford Moor. Upon the north side
of which pass lyeth the lands of the Lairdship of Castle-
hill, whereon stands the Castle of Dursdeer upon another
pass, called the Well-path that leadeth to Crawford Moor,
which formerly pertained to the Steuarts of Dursdeer,
and of late to the Meinziesses of Castle-hill in property,
the Barons of Rothesay, of the name of Stewart, having
till of late retained the superiority of it; but now all
doth pertain to the D. of Queensberry. This Castle
hath been an indifferent strong-hold; and was, in the
days of K. Edward Langshanks, possessed by a garison
of the English for keeping that pass; and afterward, in
the reign of Edward of Carnarvan, his son, taken in by
Roger Kirkpatrick. It is now ruined, and but a small
part of it remaining.

Near to this Castle stands the parish Church of Dursdeer, where the Douglasses of the family of Queensberry
have been interred; as also those of the name of Mein-
zies, that formerly had interest in this parish, and whereof some yet have. The Church is an indifferent fabrick,

situate in a little village called Dursdeer, which of old did hold of the Archbishop of Glasgow; but the few of it not being considerable, was disponed by Archbishop Spotswood to the ministers of Dursdeer, who were sub-chanters of the Diocese of Glasgow, and members of the Chapter. The church is at the presentation of the D. of Queensberry. About a mile or somewhat more, is the Barony and Place of Enoch, which did formerly belong to the Meinzieses of Weem, and of late to another succession of that name. The whole parish of Dursdeer, excepting this Barony of Enoch, on both sides of the river, pertains to the D. of Queensberry. Over against Enoch, near to the bridge of Drumlanrig, is situate the Castle of Drumlanrig, a princely and pleasant habitation, and like to be more so, being the dwelling-place of the D. of Queensberry. The original, rise, and steps of ascent of which family, is to be given in by his Grace's direction, with his other titles and heraldry. Above the Castle of Drumlanrig lyeth the Barony of Drumlanrig, about three miles up the river on the south side, where it marcheth with that part of the parish of Kirkbride.

The fifth parish, in the Presbytery of Penpont, is the parish of Penpont itself, divided on the east side from the parish of Keir by the river Scarr; and on the south and south-west side, from the parish of Tinron; on the north side, it is divided from Dursdeer by a little rivulet, called the Park Burn, or Tibber's Burn; on the north-west side, it reaches as far as Sanquhar and above; and lyeth in lenth ten miles and above from the Church, which stands at the east end of the parish. This parish marcheth with the parishes of Dursdeer, Kirkbride, and some parts of Sanquhar; and on the north-east side, it is divided by the river of Nith from the parish of Morton, on the north side of Nith. It is denominate Penpont, from a penny payed at this place for building and upholding of a wooden bridge over Nith betwixt Penpont and Morton, long since ruined, near to a village called Thornhill. At this Church is the seat of the Presbytery.

On the north side of this parish, near to Drumlanrig, is the Castle of Tibbers, formerly a strong-hold; but now totally ruined, there being no place for habitation in or near it. By whom it was built, or by whom it was ruined, it is not certain. It hath been situate in a promontory, reaching out to a narrow point, compassed about with the river Nith, and upon high ground. It hath had very strong outworks upon the south part of it. Tradition also holds it out, that it was garisoned by the English in the time of Langshanks, and taken by Wallace, who, by burning a kill, drew the garison out of the castle for stopping of the fire, and then entred in with a party that lay in ambush near it, and possessed it himself. But whether the Castle was burned by him at that time, is uncertain; this is certain, that it is now overgrown with thickets. Here was also a Barony, called Ahengashell, that did belong to a family of the name of Maitland, now extinct. Now the whole parish, except a few small heritages, belongs to the D. of Queensberry, the most considerable of which is the Lairdship of Eccles, belonging to a linage of the name of Maitland. The rest of the heritages are but small interests. In the bounds of this land of Eccles, there is a loch, called the Dowloch, of old resorted unto with much superstition, as medicinal both for men and beasts, and that with such ceremonies as are shrewdly suspected to have been begun with witchcraft; and increased afterward, by magical directions for bringing of a cloth, or somewhat that did relate to the bodies of men and women, and a shackle or teather belonging to a cow or horse; and these being cast into the loch, if they did float, it was taken for a good omen of recovery, and a part of the water carried to the patient, though to remote places, without saluting or speaking to any they met by the way. But if they did sink, the recovery of the party was hopeless. This practice was of late much curbed and restrained; but since the discovery of many medicinal fountains near to the place, the vulgar, holding that it may be as medicinal as these are, at this time begin to reassume their former practice.

Next to this parish of Penpont, lyeth the parish of Tinron, divided, on the north side of it, from Penpont by a little river called Scarr; and on the east side, by the water of Chinnell; and on the south side, by a ridge of hills running to the west end of it, where it marcheth with Galloway. This parish is divided into two parts by a little river, called Chinnell, which springs out of a hill, in Galloway, and runs through this parish, and at the east end of it, where it runneth into Scarr, and both are called Scarr, Chinnell loseth its name. The D. of Queensberry hath the superiority of this parish, and a considerable part also of it in property. The rest of it pertains to severall gentlemen, as Macqueystoun, and severall other tenements to the Laird Wilson of Crogline, on the south side of Chinnell; Peinyirie, and other tenements, to a gentleman of the name of Douglass descended of the family of Drumlanrig, on the north side; thirdly, Istenhouse on the south side, and Killwarren on the north side of Chinnell, both pertaining to John Douglass of Istenhouse.

Near to Istenhouse, on the north side of Chinnel,

L

stands the Kirk of Tinron, builded near to the Barony
of Aird, pertaining to Sir Robert Grierson of Lagg,
Knight; in the bounds of which Barony is the steep hill,
called the Dune of Tinron, of a considerable height, upon
the top of which there hath been some habitation or fort,
as is to be perceived by the ruines and outworks of it;
but it is not known by whom it was erected and inhabited,
whether by the Romans, or by the Scots and Picts. There
have been in ancient times, on all hands of it, very thick
woods and great about that place, which made it the
more inaccessible; unto which K. Robert Bruce is said
to have been conducted by Roger Kirkpatrick of Closburn, after they had killed the Cumin at Drumfreiss,
which is nine miles from this place, whereabout it is probable that he did abide for some time thereafter. And
it is reported, that, during his abode there, he did often
divert to a poor man's cottage, named Brownrig, situate
in a small parcell of stony ground, incompassed with
thick woods, where he was content sometimes with such
mean accommodation as the place could afford. The poor
man's wife being advised to petition the King for som-
what, was so modest in her desires, that she sought no
more but security for the croft in her husband's possession, and a liberty of pasturage for a very few cattle of
different kinds on the hill, and the rest of the bounds.
Of which priviledge that ancient family, by the injury
of time, hath a long time been, and is now deprived; but
the croft continues in the possession of the heirs and suc-
cessours lineally descended of this Brownrig and his wife;
so that this family, being more ancient then rich, doth
yet continue in the name, and, as they say, retains the
old charter.

The next to the parish of Tinron, is the parish of
Glencairne, bounded on the north side with a ridge of

hills, which divides it from Tinron; on the west side, it is divided from some places of the parishes of Dalry and Carsfairn, in Galloway; on the south side, with a part of the parish of Dinscore; and on the south-west side, by a part of the parish of Balmaclellan, in Galloway; and on the north-east side, by a ridge of mountains, which divides it from the parish of Kire.

This parish was of old a Mensal Kirk of the Bishoprick of Glasgow, but now at the donation of the D. of Queensberry, who is the superiour to the lands of it. This parish is large, and lyeth on both sides of a little river, called Kairn, whence it hath its denomination, which runneth from three several fountains in Galloway; the first, on the south side, called Castlefairn Water; the second, in the middle, called Craigdaroch Water, upon the brink of which stands the house of the Laird of Craigdarroch, Ferguson; the third rivulet, on the north side, is called Dowhat Water, where stands the dwelling-place of a linage of the name of M'Gachen, descended of one M'-Gachen, a private standart-bearer in the Bruce's wars, and doth yet continue in the name. These three rivulets having run each of them severall miles, do all three meet in one water at Moniaive, a Burgh of Barony, having an usefull weekly mercat, and some fairs. These three rivulets conjoined make the river Kairn. The parish, by the running of the water, running six miles downwards, is divided into two parts, one in each side; and thereafter, running on the east part of it, it divides Glenkairn from Dinscore; and thereafter running by the parish of Holywood, it divides Nidesdale from Galloway, and continueth its course by the parishes of Irongray and Teregglis, in Galloway, till it come to the Colledge of Lincluden, where it falls in with Nith.

A little beneath Moniaive, in this parish, stands the

Church of Glencarne, situate at the foot of an high hill, called the Dune of Shankcastle; near to which also stands the Castle of Glencarne, anciently the dwelling-place of the noble family of the Cuninghames, Earles of Glencarne, who being superiour to the whole parish, excepting a Barony or two, did divide the property amongst his jackmen for the greater part of it, into several tenements, bearing the name of the first occupants, which denominations, though the lands now be possessed by those of other names, yet they do still retain as at first, as Blackstown, Inglistown, Crawfordtown, Stewartown, Gilmorestown, Gordonstown, Garriokstown, and some others more; and it is probable that other places had the like denomination, though now changed. At the disposition of the superiority of this parish, the Earle of Glencarne did reserve the superiority of one room, called Nether Kirkcudbright, which he yet retains; and at the disposition of his own property, a little know, near the Castle of Glencarne, which Castle, with a considerable part of the parish, doth now pertain to Robert Laurie of Maxeltoun, Baron of Straith, which makes him capable of electing, and being elected, a Commissioner for the Parliament.

Near to this Castle, in the year 1651, when King Charles the Second had marched with his army to England, the loyal nobility and gentry of Nidesdale and Annandale being met for hasting out recruits of horse and foot for his Majestie's service, were assaulted by an English commander, one Major Scot, son to the famous brewer's clerk, Thomas Scot, a stickling member of the Rump Parliament of England, and one of the regicides, who, after his Majestie's Restitution, did receive the reward of a bold and bloudy traitour. Albeit this Major Scot was commander of fourteen score of experienced horsemen, yet the noblemen and gentlemen did resolve valiantly to abide their charge, though much inferior in number, and by a party of thirty-six or forty horse, commanded by Robert Fergusson of Craigdarroch, the English forlorn-hope, being a greater number, was stoutly and resolutely charged, broken, and beaten into their body, with the loss of severall of the English, and none of his party. Thereafter the noblemen and gentlemen, being led by Sir John Charteris of Ampfeild, Knight, did charge the body of the English, when it came up; but being inferiour in number, and many of their souldiers being not weel trained, they were forced to retire. The Master of Herris then, and of late the Earle of Nidsdale, was wounded by a shot in the arm; and though some of the English, yet none of the loyal party were killed in the fight; but some were killed in the retreat, who being denied quarters, because they could not instruct themselves to be commissionate officers or listed souldiers, were barbarously murdered, among which a young gentleman, Robert Maxwell of Tinnell, was one. Some others of quality being and avowing themselves souldiers, had quarter granted them, and were taken prisoners.

On the south side of Nith lyeth the parish of Kire, of old a pendicle of the Abbacy, and a part of the parish of Holywood, and since the Reformation, served by a substitute, who supplied both places in the absence of the minister; but lately divided from it, and erected in a parish by itself, and afterwards annexed to the Presbytery of Penpont. This parish is divided from Tinron and Penpont, upon the west part of it, by the waters of Chinnell and Scarr; and on the south part, by a ridge of mountains from Glencarne; and on the north side, by the rivers of Scarr and Nith from the parish of Dalgarno;

and on the east, from the parish of Dinscore by Alintoun Burn. It is a place fertile for corns and cattell, and richly stored with wood. The upper part of it belongs to John Grierson of Kepinoch, and some tenements that pertain to the Earle of Nithsdale. The nether part of it pertains to John Grierson of Berjarge, and several other heritours. Here is a deep loch, called the Loch of Kilbread, in a place pertaining to the Laird of Lagg; but the water is not reputed medicinal.

Ninthly, There is the parish of Morton, belonging of old to the noble Earles of Morton, and from which they have their title; a small parish; sometime one of the churches of Kelso, but now at the presentation of the Duke of Queensberry. It is, on the north-west side, divided from Dursdeer by the water of Carren; on the west side, by the river of Nith from the parish of Penpont; on the south and south-east side, from the parish of Dalgarno and Closeburn by the water of Campell; and on the east and north-east side, from Crawford Lindsay, in Clidesdale. The whole parish, excepting two small tenements, pertains to the D. of Queensberry. On the south side of this parish, near to a little village, called Thornhill, there is erected a Burgh of Regality, called New Dalgarno, where there is a weekly mercat, and four fairs in the year; at which Burgh is the publick meeting-place for jurisdiction of the Regality of Drumlanrig, called the Regality of New Dalgarno, where criminal and civil courts are holden by the Baillie of the Regality, as occasion requires. The parish Church, by recommendation from the Archbishop of Glasgow, after a perambulation, for many weighty reasons, is recommended to be erected at or near this place.

On the north side of this parish stands the old Castle of Morton, which of old hath been a very strong-hold;

but it is not certainly known by whom it was built at first. It was kept by Sir Tho. Randulph, E. of Murray, in the minority of David Bruce, and afterwards suffered to go to ruine by the Earles of Morton, who had other castles to take care of. Near to this Castle, there was a park built by Sir Thomas Randulph on the face of a very great and high hill, so artificially, that, by the advantage of the hill, all wild beasts, such as Deer, Harts, and Roes, and Hares, did easily leap in, but could not get out again ; and if any other cattle, such as Cows, Sheep, or Goats, did voluntarily leap in, or were forced to it, it is doubted if their owners were permitted to get them out again.

Tenthly, There are the united parishes of Dalgarno and Closeburn, both divided, on the west and north-west side, from the parish of Closeburn by the rivulet of Cam-pell ; and on the south and south-east side, from the pa-rish of Kirkmaho ; and on the north and north-east side, by the rivulet of Brain, springing out of Queensberry Hill, a great hill, from whence the Duke hath his title, which conjoining with another rivulet, called Keeple, makes the water of Ay, which divides from the parish of Kirkmichael. In the upper part of it, that part of Dal-garno, called Keeple Water, consists of four rooms, per-taining to the Duke of Queensberry, more fertile for cat-tel then for corns. Below that part of Dalgarno, there lyeth an eight pound land, in the parish of Closburn, pertaining to the D. of Queensberry, and a five pound land, belonging to the Laird of Cowhill, and a fourty-shilling land, belonging to Captain John Alison Baillie of the Regality of Drumlanrig, all divided from Kirk-michael by the water of Ay. A part of the parish of Dalgarno, 'ng along the river Nith, hath in it the lands of Templeland and Kirkland of Dalgarno, where the Kirk stands, now ruined; and below is the five-pound land of Schaws, the ten-merk land of Kirkpatrick and Liftingstone, where stands the Chappel of Kilpatrick, called *Cella Patricii ;* next unto which, down the river, is a ten-pound land, pertaining to the Baron of Closburn, where hath been a Chappel, and a trench for keeping of a pass at that place, which ten-pound land marches with the lands of Clawghries, pertaining to John Johnston; and the lands of Over and Nether Algirth, which are the utmost extent of Dalgarno. On the north west side of Closburn and Dalgarno, there is an eight-pound land of Newtoun, pertaining in property to Sir Robert Dalyell of Glenay, where is an excellent quarry of free-stone; above which is the ten-pound land of Ahenleck, pertaining to the Laird of Closburn, partly for corn, and partly for pasturage.

Lastly, There is the parish of Closburn, lying in the middest of Dalgarno. In that part of Closburn, towards the water of Ay, by which it is incompassed, is a fourty-pound land, pertaining to Thomas Kirkpatrick of Closburn, an ancient family, and Chef of that name, having a charter from Alexander, K. of Scots, granted to Ivon Kirkpatrick, of the lands and Barony of Closburn, before witnesses: *Bondington Cancellario, Rogero de Quency, Waltero filio Alani Senescallo Justiciario Scotiæ, Joanne de Maccuswell Camerario, Rogero Avenell, David Marescallo, Thoma filio Hamil., David de Lindsay, Rogero filio Glay, Roberto de Menyers,* dated at Edinburgh, the 15th day of August, and of the said King's reign the eighteenth year. Moreover, the said Laird, for his arms and ensign-armorial, bears *argent* a St Andrew's Cross *azure* on a sheaf of the second three cushions *Or ;* above the shield, an helmet befitting his degree, mantled *Geuls* doubled *argent.* Next, is placed on a torse for his crest, a hand holding a dagger, distilling drops of bloud *proper;* the motto in an escrole, *I make sure :* Which crest and motto was given by Robert the Bruce, K. of Scots, to Roger Kirkpatrick, upon his killing of the Cumin at the Chappel of Drumfreiss. This parish of old was a pendicle of the Abbacy of Kelso; but now is annexed to the Bishoprick of Galloway, as Dalgarno is to Edinburgh; but the Laird of Closburn is patron to both churches united.

Upon the west side of this parish, Closburn Church is situate, a little fabrick, but well built; near unto which is the Loch of Closburn, upon the east side whereof stands the dwelling-house of the Lairds of Closburn, which hath been a considerable strength of old, by bringing the Loch of Closburn about it, whence it is called Closburn, because inclosed with water or burn. This loch is of great deepness, and was measured on the ice eight acres, in the midst of a spacious bog. The fish of this loch are for the most part eels, with some great pikes, who, for lack of food, eat up all the young. At the side of this loch, there is of late discovered a fountain of medicinal waters, which, as Moffet Well, doth gild silver, and produce the other effects thereof. It is esteemed in dry weather stronger then Moffet Well, by reason of the greater abundance of sulphur putridum, sal ammoniacum, and antimony there; so that one cannot digg in a great part of the bog, but the water hath such a tang as the well. A further account of it is left to the physicians, when they shall have the conveniency to make a triall of it. There is also, within a mile of Closburn-house, another loch, called Loch Atrick, but little remarkable about it. About the Place of Closburn, and in other places of the Barony, is some store of oak wood.

There is here also two great Kairns; the one in the Moorfield, far from stones; the other in the Infeild, near unto them; whence the bounds is called Ahenkairn, which surely are two ancient monuments, although an account of them cannot be given.

Nithsdale is divided into two Wards or Divisions. The Upper Ward consisteth of eleven Parishes of the Classis or Presbytery of Penpont, which, by the union of two of them, viz. Dalgarno and Closburn of old, and by the late annexation of Kirkconnall to Sanquhar, do now make but nine parishes; but, notwithstanding the union and annexation foresaid, every parish is described here by itself.

No. VIII.

DEDICATION OF SYMSON'S TRIPATRIARCHICHON.

To the Right Honourable and truly Noble James Earl of Galloway, Lord Stewart of Gairlies and Glasserton.

My Lord,

This poem was written in that part of the kingdom, from whence your Lordship has the honourable title of Earl; and wherein your Lordship's predecessors, for several generations, have had, not only ample possessions, but also great power and authority.

And here, my Lord, I have adventured to give an account of several of your Lordship's famous ancestours; and although, no doubt, your Lordship can give a better, yet I presume it will not be altogether unuseful for your

Lordship, were it but to help and refresh your Lordship's memory ; seeing, in things of this nature, the names of persons and places, together with the particular designations, of times and years, are very apt to slip out of the memory of such as are endued with the best portion thereof. Nor will it, I suppose, be unacceptable to several others of the name of Stewart, who are Cadets of your Lordship's family, to see that in print, which perhaps might otherwise fall into oblivion. I conceive also, that this account may in some respect gratify all others, who are curious inquirers into the pedigrees of our ancient families ; and I think it will displease none, except such as have a perfect antipathy at the whole surname of Stewart ; and I suppose very few of such, if any, will be found in the kingdom of Scotland, it being the surname of our Kings for many generations.

I shall not presume to trace your Lordship's family up to its original, or show who was the first that had the possession and stile of Gairlies, our records and documents being herein defective ; but sure I am, it may be made evident by authentick records, charters, and documents, yet extant, that your Lordship's family is very antient, which may fully appear by what followeth, viz.

Sir Walter Stewart, one of your Lordship's predecessors, got from King Robert Bruce the Baronie of Dalswintoun, in Nithesdale, for good and faithful service, as a charter, yet in being, testifys. As also the said Sir Walter had from his nephew, John Randulph, Earl of Murray, in the reign of King David Bruce, a charter of confirmation of the Baronie of Gairlies. Likeas, it is plain from the archives of the kingdom, in the reign of K. James II. and III., that Sir William Stewart of Dalswintoun and Gairlies had to his eldest son, Sir Alexander Stewart, his successor ; Walter Stewart, of whom

Stewart of Tonderghie, in the parish of Whithern, is descended ; and Sir Thomas Stewart, to whom his father, Sir William, with consent of his son and heir, Sir Alexander, gave the lands of Minto and Morbottle, in Teviotdale ; from which family of Minto is descended the Right Honourable the Lord Blantyre, in Scotland. Likeas, from this family of Minto, there were descended two loyal brethren, living in the reign of K. Charles I. viz. Sir William and Sir Robert Stewarts, one of which was predecessor to the Right Honourable the Lord Montjoy, in the kingdom of Ireland. From this family of Minto also, are descended several of the name of Stewart, viz. Fintilloch and Barhills, both in the parish of Penygham ; Stewart of Shambellie, near Dumfries ; Stewart of Heisilside, in the Parish of Douglas, and Sheriffdome of Clydsdale, with several others.

It is also evident, that Sir Alexander Stewart of Gairlies adher'd to that gallant, but unfortunate, Prince James III. at Bannockburn, and was knighted both by James III. and his son James IV. The same or another Sir Alexander was killed at the fatal battel of Flouden, anno 1513, under the royal standart of James IV., which Sir Alexander had issue, one son and nineteen daughters, all married to considerable Barons, as the list, yet extant, declares.

Sir Alexander Stewart of Gairlies, in the reign of K. James V., was one of the ambassadours from that prince to K: Henry VIII. of England, and had to wife Margaret Dunbar, Lady Clugston, daughter to the Laird of Mochrum, and sister to Gavin Dunbar, Archbishop of Glasgow, and Archbald Dunbar, first Laird of Baldone ; which Margaret Dunbar had also to him a second son, of whom came the Laird of Phisgil, in the parish of Glasserton ; and from Phisgil is descended Stewart of Livingstoun, in the parish of Balmaghie, in the Stewartrie of Kirkcudburgh, and several others, both in the Stewartrie of Kirkcudburgh, and Sherifdome of Wigton.

This Sir Alexander had by another venter severall other children, from whom are the Stewarts of Croscherie, and Clarie, of which family of the Clarie was the famous Colonel William Stewart, (a valiant and stately man, whom I have frequently seen,) who being a Colonel in the great Gustavus Adolphus's army, made a great purchase, which, after his decease, came to that obliging gentleman, your Lordship's uncle, William Stewart of Castle-Stewart, by vertue of his marrying Elizabeth Gordon, grandchild to the said Colonel William Stewart of Castle-Stewart.

In the minority of King James the VI., Sir Alexander Stewart of Gairlies offer'd to combat with that daring hero, Kircaldie of Grange, governour of the Castle of Edinburgh, who gave a chalenge to any of the adverse party that durst fight him; which Sir Alexander was afterwards killed at Stirling with Matthew, Earl of Lennox, Regent and grandfather to King James the VI. Another of your Lordship's ancestors was Sir Alexander Stewart, commonly designed the White Knight of Gairlies; he married Christian Douglass, daughter to the Baron of Drumlangrig, by whom he had issue, Alexander, your Lordship's great-grandfather, who was born about the year 1580, and created first Lord Gairlies about the year 1609, and Earl of Galloway, Lord Stewart of Gairlies and Glassertoun, about the year 1622. The said Sir Alexander had also a second son, commonly designed of Mains, (in the parish of Whithern,) who, by marrying   Stewart, heiress of Burrough, in Orkney, became Laird of Burrough, whose grandchild and successor is the present Honourable Sir Archibald

Stewart of Burrough, Baronet ; the which William of
Maines and Burrough had also another son, called William, who was adjutant to the famous and loyal Marques
of Montrose, at the battel of Philiphaugh ; which adjutant hath left issue, the present accomplish'd and honourable Lieutennant-General Stewart, famous both at home
and abroad.

My Lord,

I do not pretend to be an exact genealogist, I leave
that to heralds and to such as have more leasure, and
better opportunities to prosecute that studie. I have
only here collected some gleanings of your Lordship's
family, and some (and but some) of the Cadets from it,
and have done this that it may be only as an introduction to my great design in this dedication, which is, that
so I may make a publick acknowledgment of the particular favours which I have receiv'd from your Lordship's
family, viz. from your Lordship's grandfather, your Lordship's father, and your Lordship.

As for your Lordship's grandfather, James Earl of
Galloway, he was a proper stately person, and most courteous and affable, so that the meanest in the whole countrey might easily have got access to him, to make their
complaint to him upon any account, wherein they con-
ceiv'd they were injur'd ; and yet, in the mean time, he
knew well enough to keep his due distance, and maintain
the dignity of his character. The whole countrey, both
gentry and others, had an intire affection for him, and
were ready to attend him, whenever he called for them,
which was sufficiently verifyed in the insurrection, Nov.
1666, which began in the Stewartrie of Kirkcudburgh.
Upon his advertisement, the whole gentry of the Shire
of Wigtoun flock'd immediately to him ; so that if those

people had come into that countrey, they had met with a sufficient force to oppose them. He was very just in all his bargains, so that I never heard any person lay any thing of the contrary to his charge. He was so loyal to his prince, that he was severely fined for it in the time of the English usurpation.

He was abundantly respectful to the ministers in that countrey, and particularly to myself; so that when he rode betwixt his two ordinary dwelling-houses, Glasserton and the Clarie, my house being in the way, and almost equaly distant, his Lordship was pleas'd to honour me so far, as to call and alight at my house, and to invite me to his, where I have been kindly entertain'd. I had occasion to uplift a considerable sum yearly payable out of his Baronie of Clugstoun, and when the term of payment was elaps'd, I never desir'd a precept from him, but he immediately signed it; yea, and many times when I could not conveniently go for it, if I sent but my servant with a letter for it, it was immediately sent to me, and directed to his chamberlain, who payed me always thankfully upon demand, without the least defalcation.

As also did your Lordship's father, Earl Alexander, with whom I had the honour to be a condisciple at the university. He was also greatly respected by the gentry of the whole countrey. He was just and upright in all his dealings. I remember one day, when calling and alighting at my house, (as his father us'd to do,) he, among other discourse, took occasion to speak very severely against persons, who, by quirks and tricks of law, refus'd to pay their predecessors' debts, solemnly asserting, that if any man would come, and make it appear, that any of his numerous ancestors were justly owing him anything, he would pay it to the least sixpence.

And I remember, that, when I was in that countrey,

I have heard it oftimes boasted of, that there was never a just creditor of the family of Galloway that was a loser by having that family their debitor. As he was kind and courteous to all persons, so there was one act of kindness to myself which I cannot forget, viz. In the year 1679, when things were come to that hight, that the publick owning of us was almost look'd upon as a crime, and I for my own safety was necessitate to retire to a quiet lurking place, his Lordship accidentaly lighted on me, took me home with him to his house, and kindly entertained me there.

As for yourself, my Lord, (although I was remov'd from that countrey before your father's decease, yet) your Lordship was pleased to call for my son, and to give him the charge of two of your Lordship's brethren at the university; and they (such was their good nature and disposition) had an intire affection for him, (which yet continues,) and carried themselves very respectively towards him. And your Lordship has at all occasions given sufficient instances of your kindnesses to him, which I hope he will be always sensible of, being never, as far as I know, charg'd with the least ingratitude.[1]

[1] The precise date of Symson's removal from Kirkinner has not been ascertained. It seems probable that printing was not the first trade to which he turned his attention, after settling in Edinburgh. He describes himself as a *Merchant Burgess* of that city, in an advertisement prefixed to an edition of M'Kenzie's *Observations on the Statutes*, printed by him in 1698. Watson, in the preface to his *History of Printing*, gives an account of the printing-houses of Edinburgh, and informs us, that, " In 1700, Mr Mathew Sympson, a student of divinity, set up a small *house*; but he designing to prosecute his studies, left the *house* to his father Mr Andrew, one of the suffering clergy, who kept up the house till about a year ago that he died." Watson's work was published in 1713, from which it would appear, that Symson must have died early in 1712. His library was disposed of by public sale after his death. The catalogue was printed under the title of " *Bibliotheca Symsoniana*; a catalogue of the vast collection of books, in the library of the late reverend and learned Mr Andrew Symson. Edinburgh, printed in the year 1712. 4to. pp. 34."— ED.

These acts of kindness received from your Lordship's family, I think, merit a publick acknowledgment, which, by dedicating this poem, (such as it is,) I have taken the occasion in some measure to perform.

And now, my Lord, I have no more to add, but my fervent prayer to God, to bless the ancient familie of the Stewarts, and the dutiful Cadets thereof; and that God would multiply his blessings, both spiritual and temporal, upon your Lordship, your Lordship's vertuous lady, and hopefull children; and that your Lordship's family may allways be found faithfull servants to God, loyal to their soveraigns, patriots to their countrey, and thereby they may find favour in the sight of God and man; this is and shall be the unfeigned prayer of,

My noble Lord,

Your Lordship's most humble, and most obedient
Servant, in all duty,

ANDREW SYMSON.

No. IX.

Preface to Symson's Tripatriarchichon.

English poesie being now come to a great height, by the elaborat poems of Cowley, Dryden, Blackmore, and several others of late, my reader, when he sees a poem that dares appear in publick after them, may perhaps be inclin'd to conjecture, that this must, if not equal, yet at least in some measure resemble or be like theirs. Upon which consideration, he may be perswaded to ad-

M

venture on the perusal of it ; but if he knew or thought otherwise, he would not so much as allow it the favour of a superficial glance.

Well then, to undeceave my Reader, and to deal plainly with him, before he read any further, I would have him know, that although this poem do but now appear in print, yet it is not new ; the greatest part of it being written more than thirty, yea, and some part of it more than fourty years since. Moreover, it was writen in a remote part of the kingdom, where the author's books were not many, and his books of English poems very few ; having never seen, much less read, any English poems, except those of Quarles, Wild, and two or three more. Furthermore, the author had not there the acquaintance of any one that did in the least pretend to any skil in English poesie.

So that the author does not in the least expect to be classed with our famous modern English poets. No, no ; the height of his ambition is to be ranked *inter minores poetas ;* or if that seem too bigg, he is content to be listed *inter minimos,* providing ordinary ballad-makers, countrey rhythmers, mercenary epitaph-mongers, and several others of that tribe, be wholy excluded the number.

It will sufficiently satisfy me, if this pass among the judicious for a tolerably good trotting poem ; for it was never my design, nor did ever my ambition prompt me to it, to set up for a courser, or, with Icarus, to aspire to high flights ; foreseeing, that I might so quickly run myself out of breath, or catch a fall, which would have hinder'd me to attain my design'd end, to which, by trotting on, I have at length come.

And now, Reader, if, after this fair advertisment, thou wilt yet adventure to peruse it, upon thy own peril be it; for whether it will please thee, or displease thee, I know not. However, I think it will not be amiss to give an account of the occasion of my first writing it.

My natural genius being something delighted with this jingling art, on a time (and I cannot tell how it came in my head to do it) I turn'd a passage or two of the Book of Genesis into English verse, without any kind of fiction of things or persons; so that what I had done was little more than a bare turning of the English prose into English verse. A little while after, I did the like with two or three more. After that, being something pleas'd with my own fancy, (as most men, as well as I, are with theirs,) it came into my thought to turn the whole Book of Genesis, at least so much of it as concerned Abram, Isaac, and Jacob, into verse, and to call it by the name of *Tripatriarchichon;* whereupon I provided a general preface, and an introduction; and afterwards at several times, as my other occasions would allow, did the like with several passages, that I had not formerly meddl'd with. This was not done in order, but here and there, as my present fancy prompted me, inserting also sometimes short explications of the text, allusions, meditations, similies, reflexions, and such digressions, as at the time occurr'd to me, and which I then thought pertinent enough to be inserted. At length I gathered together the scatter'd parcells, filling up the blanks, that, by supplying what was defective, I might make the whole joyn and hang together, and thus at last I brought it to a period.

So that this poem being compos'd at several times, and not in order, as it now appears, the Reader may easily perceave that it is not all of a piece. In many places, he will find such lines as the meanest poetaster might readily write; in other places, perhaps, there may

be found some few lines, here and there, more brisk and
lively, of which a better poet, than I could ever pretend
to be, need not be ashamed.

It being thus written at several times, no wonder, I
say, that it is not all of a piece; for I was not always in
the same humour; for although my temper and constitution does much incline me to an unconcernedness with
the vicissitudes of the world, as not to be puft up with
its summer blossoms, or dejected with its nipping frosts,
which I remember once occasioned me to write the following lines :—

> I do protest, I scorn to be a slave
> Unto the world. What! shall the subject have
> Dominion ov'r his prince ? No, no, I deem
> The world to be my foot-ball; and esteem
> The greatest courtesie that it can do,
> Scarce worth enjoying for a day or two.
> Sometimes it smiles indeed; but then that flow'r
> Doth seldom last much longer than an hour.
> Most times it frowns; what then ? for so can I,
> Yea more, despise the chief discourtesie
> That it can do. Whenever I project
> Heroick actions, if they fail, defect
> Shall nev'r dismay me; if they thrive, my Maker
> Shall get the praise of what I'm made partaker.
> I'll still expect the worst, and then I'm sure,
> By his assistance, I may well endure
> The spight of fortune; why ? because my cross
> Being thus expected, will not be a loss,
> But rather an advantage. O Supreme
> Of all the Universe, send forth a beam
> Of thy resplendent rays upon my soul,
> This soul of mine, that so I may controul
> This brittle world; and then I shall be blest
> To do indeed, what here I do protest.

Yet I have not so much of the Stoick in me as to be
altogether insensible of such things as frequently come

to pass; nor am I so much possest with *their apathy*, as to be never in the least mov'd at *come what will come.* No; my religion obliges me to *Rejoyce with them that do rejoyce, and to weep with them that weep.* This Christian sympathy did many times really affect me, when I considered the state and condition of things, which were very various, in the times wherein this poem was written; all which being considered, it is no wonder that the poem itself should not always appear to be of the same strain.

And thus I have given an account of the occasion that gave rise to this poem, and the manner how it was written. But I fancie there will be faults found with it, being written.

Some perhaps will alledge that I have too much of the satyr, when I declaim against vice and immorality. But to this I answer, That when vice and immorality is not only publickly practis'd, but also generally applauded, I think it then high time for all good men to level their sharpest arrows against it. The Apostle St Paul will have Titus to rebuke the Cretians sharply for their lying, barbarities, cruelties, ill-nature, and idleness, &c. Tit. i. 13, which I conceive gives me a sufficient warrant for what I have done. The most cautious physician, when he meets with a stubborn disease in a strong constitution, makes no scruple to lay aside the gentle prescripts of Galen, and make use of the more powerfull ones of Paracelsus; and yet many times he finds the stubbornness of the disease resist those rugged applications; as I fear (such is the perversness of this generation) all our sharpest satyrs and bitter invectives will be found too too weak to procure a thorough reformation.

Some again perhaps will blame me for exposing the male-treatments, that in those days we met with; but

since I say nothing but what is literally true, I cannot
see how any can blame me for finding fault with that
which no good man can justify, especially considering
severall circumstances, which will the better appear by
this short, yet true and impartial history of that time
and place, where we then had our residence. I say, where
we then had our residence; for I do hereby restrict myself to the Presbyteries of Wigton and Stranrawer; the
first whereof consists of nine parishes, and the other con-
sisted then of eight, and were united *pro tempore* into one
Presbyterie, for the better exercise of discipline; both
these Presbyteries contain a large tract of ground, being
more than thirtie miles of length, and in some places
more than twentie miles of breadth; I say, I restrict
myself only to those bounds, where I liv'd about the
space of twenty-three years, that so, by giving a short
and true account thereof, I might insert nothing but
what I knew *ex certa scientia,* which is as followeth.

In the beginning of the year 1663, being invited to
go to that countrey to supply the vacant congregations
there, upon our arrival we found several parishes, not
only *vacantes,* but *vocantes,* desiring and earnestly solli-
citing that ministers might be sent to supply their va-
cancies. I do not assert that we had a formal and explicit call from the parishioners, (which although sometimes it may tend *ad bene, aut melius esse Ecclesiæ,* yet
I never thought that it was requisit *ad esse Ecclesiæ;*
and this my sentiment is, if I am not mistaken, agreeable to those of Presbyterians themselves, which I think
I am able to demonstrat from their own acts; but this
is not my present business;) I say, though we had not
a formal and explicit call, yet we had it virtually, and
upon the matter; for after we had several Lord's days
preached in our respective congregations for which we

were designed, (seven Lord's days I am sure for my own part,) our edicts served and duly execute, the representatives of the parish attended on our ordinations, and the generallty of the parish came to our solemn admissions; and thereafter waited on the ordinances under our administrations, yea, and the very members of the former sessions concurr'd with us, and assisted us in the exercise of discipline, and rectifying such affairs as was incumbent to them, after the old manner. Our admissions and entry being so peaceable, so orderly, and so generaly assented to, I cannot think that any of our number was in the least tempted to procure a fraught to transport themselves to America. Sure I am, our admissions then were as peaceably and orderly, as many that succeeded in these places since 1689 can boast of; and more peaceably than the admissions of many in several parts of the kingdom, which might be easily instanc'd, if need were.

As for those few that were dissenters, we us'd all peaceable and Christian methods to gain them; so that when the commander of the forces, that lay in the Stewartrie of Kirkcudburgh, (for there were none of them in our countrey,) wrote to us to send him a list of them, we absolutely refused him, and sent two of our number, yet living, to signify the same to him; upon which account we were complained of as enemies to the government, and obstructers of the settlement of the peace of the countrey. And by this our deportment, there was such a general harmony betwixt us and our parishoners, that, in the latter end of the year 1666, when there was an insurrection, which terminated at Pentland-hills, there were only two persons (and one of them was a servant to the other) that were present with those people; and there were no other persons in that countrey that ever I could hear of, though diligent search was made by the government thereanent, that were found to have had any hand in it.

It is not my present business to give an account of the true causes of that insurrection, or to inquire whether it were only accidental, upon the account that one of Sir James Turner's souldiers was wounded by Barscob, at the Old Clachan, or whether it was contrived sometime before. But in regard I have seen a manuscript journal of that short campaign, written by a very intelligent and inquisitive person, who was present with them all the time, and gives a particular account of all the circumstances, betwixt the 15th of November in the morning, till the 28th day at even, I shall only insert one passage, which I remember to have read in it, because it is something singular, and may be acceptable to some of my Readers; 'tis as followeth.

November 15th, 1666, betwixt eight and nine in the morning, one who called himself Captain Gray, being attended with several armed men, seised on Sir James Turner, at Dumfreis, together with a coffer of his, wherein were baggs of money, cloaths, and papers; whereupon, after they had taken himself, his money, papers, horses, arms, cloaths, and linnens, they marched in hast away from thence. and came that night to Glencairn, and thence to Castle-Ferne. On the 16th, they came to the Old Clachan of Dalry, and at night Captain Gray and Sir James were lodg'd at Mr Chalmers of Watersid's house, being on the other side of the river of Kenn, not far from the Old Clachan. Captain Gray, about eleven or twelve a clock at night, being allarm'd with a report, that the Earle of Annandale, Lord Drumlangrig, and some others were coming against him, he march'd immediately, though the night was very dark and raining, and the way very bad, eight miles to Corsphairn, where having committed Sir James to the charge of sixteen horsemen, he retired with the money and luggage he had got at Dumfries, so quietly that he was never seen by any of his own party after that. My author, in his manuscript, I remember, tells, that although he made strict inquiry concerning him, yet he got no other answer from those of his own party, but that they knew nothing of him, except that he called himself Captain Gray, and that he had brought an order with him, to them all to obey him. This by the by; I shall now return to my former relation.

It pleased the King, after this, to grant an indulgence to several ministers of the Presbyterian perswasion, for which they gave their thanks judicially before the Lords of Privy Council; and after that, he granted another indulgence to several others of the same perswasion. Many ministers, of the Presbyterian perswasion also, were highly offended at their brethren's accepting of these indulgences; so that both parties not only spoke, but also wrote one against the other, as their books printed on that subject do evidently declare. Those that were displeased with the indulgence, were, I remember, in those days commonly called the Hill-men, who came first unto the skirts and mountanous parts of our countrey, and preach'd there; from thence, by degrees, they came to the very heart of the countrey, and withdrew several of our formerly orderly parishoners from us; and yet many of those in the intervals returned to us again, and back again as occasion offered. By these means such extravagancies were committed, that the government thought it high time to take notice of them; so that there were severe acts made, and proclamations issued out against those actings, which sometimes were intrusted to persons to execute, who, for politick ends,

did sometimes severely execute them; though, in the
mean time, others, for politick ends too, did connive at,
and encourage them.   We, in the mean time, forseeing
what would be the fatal consequences of putting those
acts and proclamations in full execution, us'd our outmost endeavours to ward off the blow; and by our inter-
cession and diligence in that affair, we got the penalty
most times mitigated, yea, and many times wholy taken
off; for which we got but little thanks many times from
both parties; but there were some faults, such as mur-
ders, robberies, forgeries, and crimes of that nature, that
we could not plead for; and when such persons were
punished for such and the like misdemeanours, (because
they assumed to themselves the title of the godly party,)
we were blamed for all those punishments that lighted
upon any of them, which so stirr'd up others to male-
treat us at the rate, which in this poem I sometimes do
complain of.   Now let any good Christian, or any rational man, considering our peaceable entry among them,
our Christian and ministerial deportment with them,
(for, in all the time that I was there, I do not remember
that any thing of moment was laid to the charge of any
of our number, either as to our doctrine, life, or conver-
sation,) and our acts of kindness towards them, the
odium that we met with from some persons, for our
pleading for them, and yet at length to be so male-treat-
ed by them; I say, let any good Christian, or rational
man, considering those circumstances, judge whether or
not I had not reason at that time, to insert such things
in my poem (being all matters of fact) as some persons
were in those days guilty of.

However, I must in the mean time acknowledge, that
as my lot was cast in a very pleasant place, so I had to
do with a very well-natur'd people, who, following the

example of the gentry, their landlords, payed me great deference and respect, for which people, for I hate ingratitude, I shall have a kindness as long as I breath ; so that I was for the most part free from those male-treatments that many of my brethren mett with, (towards whom my religion obliged me to have a sympathy.) I confess I was not altogether free of my own troubles, which proceeded much more from strangers than those of my own parish ; for they in the mean time were so kind to me, that, when they were advertis'd of any approaching danger, they have both by day and night advertis'd me thereof, upon which I have many times retired myself quietly into their countrey-houses, where I was lodg'd and kindly entertain'd, and so escaped the danger I might otherwise have been subject too.

'Tis probable some criticks will find fault with me for not using an uniform manner in spelling and pointing. But in regard our greatest criticks have not, for any thing I know, given us an exact standart, either for the one or the other, and these sheets being *set* by two or three *Compositars* at the same time, and each of them spelling and pointing differently, when it came to me to revise, I was not very nice in making several alterations of what they had done, knowing that I could produce sufficient authority from learn'd authors for each of them. There are, I confess, some *typographical errata* to be found, which the greatest care can hardly prevent ; but as these are easily perceived by the judicious and candid reader, so they will I hope be as easily excused. However, there is one word, which, by a mere inadvertencie, is many times wrong printed, viz. *Tripatiarchichon* for *Tripatriarchicon*, in the running-title of the even pages through several sheets, which was not observed till those sheets were wrought off.

Some again, perhaps, will find fault with the quantities of some proper names; but for that, I find that
many persons pronounce them, sometimes long, sometimes short, and I have taken the same liberty, which I
hope no man will grudge me of.

There are several words and phrases in this poem,
which will not sound well in a pure English ear. I have
examined them, and I find they are agreeable enough to
our northern dialect; and I see no reason why I may
not make use of it, when it serves my purpose, as well as
Homer, the prince of the Greek poets, who oft-times
makes use of the various dialects of the Greek language;
and was never censur'd for it (as far as I know) by any
of the severest criticks.

I shall make no further apologie, but conclude in the
words of a great man:—" If there be any errors (as
possibly there may be) in my deductives, inferences, or
applications; or if the language be in some places either
improper or obscure; or if the expression or words,
which I sometimes use, be not so full, so significant, or
proper, or delivered from amphibologies, yet I must desire the reader to take this apologie for it: It was written at leisure and broken times, and with great inter-
valls, and many times hastily, as my busie and important
imployment of another nature would give me leave, which
must needs make such breaks and chasms, and incohe-
rences, that possibly a continued uninterrupted *series* of
writing would have prevented, and carried on the *poem*
with a more equal threed."

And now, Reader, if thou art but *tolerably well pleas'd*
with it, I shall be *very well pleas'd;* but if thou be dis-
pleas'd at it, I cannot help it now, unless I should de-
stroy the whole impression, which I am not inclined to
do; but am content it run the fate of other books, to be

censur'd as peoples' fancies lead them ; and if I shall find
it meet with any sharp censure, 'tis like I shall not much
concern myself therein.   However, I am
Your humble servant in all duty,
ANDREW SYMSON.

*From my Printing-house, at the foot of the Horse-Wind,
in the Cowgate.   Feb. 16, 1705.*

No. X.

A Meditation on Death, occasioned by the Funeral of the Vertuous Lady, Agnes M'Culloch, Relict of Umquhile William Maxwell
of Murreith.

Obiit Feb. 4, 1684.   Sepulta Feb. 12, 1684.

Symson's Elegies, p. 29.

Man's life is like unto a winter's day,
Both being but short ; for, as we oft-times say,
The longest day of winter's short, being done
Oft-times before we thought it well begun.
So is man's life.   Some, newly born, do cry
An hour, (and some not that,) and then they dye ;
Some live a longer space, and do abide
Till Phæbus, with his restless steeds, doth ride
Quite through the Zodiack, and then go home
From their short pilgrimage unto the womb

Of mother earth ; some others live to see
That space of time summ'd up by ten times three ;
Some live to fourty years, and some agen
Attain to threescore ; some to threescore ten,
Yea, and some others (though they are but few)
See eightie, ere they bid the world adieu.
And yet what are these steps, or these essays
From one to eightie, but like winter days ;
Some very short, some longer than the rest,
Yet all are short when brought unto the test
Of a just judgement.   Eighty will amount
But to a winter day, if that we count
The same aright, and do exactly try
That space i' th' ballance of the Sanctuary,
And counter-ballance it with Eternity.

   Man's life is like unto a winter's day,
Being dark and cloudy ; true, some pass away
Their time in greater mirth than others do,
Yet they, believe me, have their sorrows too ;
Yea, and their sunshine of prosperity
Is like dark clouds that overspread the sky,
If but compar'd with that eternal pleasure,
That God will give the righteous without measure.

   It is decreed that ev'ry man must dy
One time or other ; there's no remedy
T' avoid the same ; death is a common debt
That all must pay ; none can be free from it.
The very bankrupt himself must pay
The same ; nor can the lawyer find a way
To shift it by ; the doctor cannot save
Himself, by all his potions, from the grave ;
Nor can the quaint philosopher invent
A medium, or produce an argument

T' enervate it ; nor can the politician
Trepan the same ; nor can the exact musician
Lull death asleep ; nor yet can the divine
Find out a way whereby he may decline
That path ; nor can the orator, with his wit,
And high-flown eloquence, escape from it.
The conqueror himself, that wins the field,
Killing ten thousands with his sword, must yield
Himself death's pris'ner ; all his force and pow'r
Cannot protract his own life for an hour.

It was the vertuous lady here that lyes
Abstracted, in this coffin, from our eyes,
That gave my low-borne, home-bred muse th' occasion
T' endite, and pen to write this meditation ;
And therefore 'twill not be amiss that I
Should, though in short, ere I conclude, apply.

Her age was great, because she liv'd to see
Her children's children to the third degree ;
Yet, notwithstanding, I am bold to say,
'Twas at the most but a short winter day.
And to proceed, although she was not vext
With quintessence of sorrow, nor perplext
With floods and seas of grief, yet still I'll say,
Her lifetime was a cloudy winter day.

She was a lady of great moderation,
A vertue slighted by this generation.

The dowrie left her by her loving spouse
She manag'd well ; she did not rant, carouse,
Or spend as many wanton widows doe ;
(And if 'twere fitting I could name them too,)
Nor did she like a niggard hoord the same,
(A fault for which some widows are to blame,)
But she improv'd it well, and did provide
For her descendants, and the poor beside.

Her house was as an alms-house, she being ready
To reach her hand forth to the poor and needy;
Yea more, I think, I need not doubt to call
Barmeal, while she dwelt there, an hospital.

    Well, that I may conclude, she now is dead;
'Tis true, death is the path that all must tread,
And therefore each of us should stand in aw
Of sin, and learn t'observe God's holy law,
And so we need not doubt, when ere we dy,
To live with God to all eternity.

ON THE UNEXPECTED DEATH OF THE VERTUOUS
   LADY, MRS JANET DALRYMPLE, LADY BALDONE,
   YOUNGER.[1]

Nupta Aug. 12. *Domum ducta Aug.* 24. *Obiit Sept.* 12.
    Sepult. Sept. 30. M.DC.LX.IX.

Dialogus inter Advenam et Servum Domesticum.

Symson's Elegies, p. 10.

    ADV. WHAT means this sudden unexpected change?
This mourning company? Sure, sure, some strange
And uncouth thing hath happen'd; Phœbus's head
Hath not been resting on the wat'ry bed
Of sea-green Thetis fourty times, since I
In *transitu* did cast my tender eye

---

    [1] This unfortunate lady was daughter to President Dalrymple.
She was seized with madness on her marriage-night, and nearly murdered her husband. It has been supposed, that her disastrous fate
suggested the idea of that beautiful romance, *The Bride of Lammer-
moor.*—Vide *Law's Memorials*, p. 226, *Note.* ED.

Upon this very place, and here did view
A troop of gallants : Iris never knew
The various colours which they did employ
To manifest and represent their joy.
Yea more ; methinks I saw this very wall
Adorn'd with emblems hieroglyphicall ;
As first, the glorious sun in lustre shine ;
Next unto it, a young and tender vine
Surround a stately elm, whose tops were crown'd
With wreaths of bay-tree reaching to the ground ;
And to be short, methinks I did espy
A pleasant, harmless, joyfull comedy.
But now (sad change, I'm sure,) they all are clad
In deepest sable, and their faces sad ;
The sun's o'reclouded, and the vine's away,
The elm is drooping, and the wreaths of bay
Are chang'd to cypress, and the comedie
Is metamorphos'd to a tragedie.
I do desire you, Friend, for to unfold
This matter to me.

    SERV. DOM.   Sir, 'tis truth you've told ;
We did enjoy great mirth, but now, ah me !
Our joyful song's turn'd to an elegie.
A vertuous lady, not long since a bride,
Was to an hopeful plant by marriage ty'd
And brought home hither.   We did all rejoyce
Even for her sake.   But presently our voice
Was turn'd to mourning, for that little time
That she'd enjoy ; she waned in her prime ;
For *Atropus*, with her impartial knife,
Soon cut her threed, and therewithall her life.
And for the time, we may it well remember,
It being in unfortunate September,

Just at the equinox ; she was cut down
In th' harvest, and this day she's to be sown,
Where we must leave her till the resurrection ;
'Tis then the saints enjoy their full perfection.

END OF THE APPENDIX.

PRINTED BY JAMES BALLANTYNE AND CO.

CPSIA information can be obtained
at www.ICGtesting.com
Printed in the USA
BVOW08s0847190617

487263BV00008B/137/P